**W9-AUS-827**

always up to date

The law changes, but Nolo is on top of it! We offer several
ways to make sure you and your Nolo products are up to date:

1 **Nolo's Legal Updater**
We'll send you an email whenever a new edition of this book
is published! Sign up at **www.nolo.com/legalupdater**.

2 **Updates @ Nolo.com**
Check **www.nolo.com/update** to find recent changes
in the law that affect the current edition of your book.

3 **Nolo Customer Service**
To make sure that this edition of the book is the most
recent one, call us at **800-728-3555** and ask one of
our friendly customer service representatives.
Or find out at **www.nolo.com**.

please note

We believe accurate, plain-English legal information should help
you solve many of your own legal problems. But this text is not a
substitute for personalized advice from a knowledgeable lawyer.
If you want the help of a trained professional—and we'll always
point out situations in which we think that's a good idea—consult
an attorney licensed to practice in your state.

NOLO

6th edition

8 Ways to
Avoid
Probate

by Mary Randolph, J.D.

SIXTH EDITION	May 2006
EDITOR	Ralph Warner
PRODUCTION	Sarah Hinman
PROOFREADER	Susie Seefelt Lesieutre
INDEXER	Michael Ferreira
PRINTING	Delta Printing Solutions, Inc.

International Standard Serial Number (ISSN)1931-0889

ISBN 1-4133-0400-1

About Our Cover
Astrid plays an integral role at Guide Dogs for the Blind
(www.guidedogs.com)—her pups become loyal helpers and
confidence-boosters to visually impaired people. In much the
same way, Nolo books and software will guide you step by
step through the unfamiliar legal tangles of life's big events.

Acknowledgments

My heartfelt thanks go to:

Jake Warner, who, as always, provided enthusiasm, support, and spot-on editing.

Denis Clifford, who gave generous and valuable help reviewing the manuscript. I am also indebted to him for the wealth of information in his own estate planning books.

Naomi Starkman, who cheerfully and doggedly helped with legal research for the first edition, and Ella Hirst, who carefully updated statutory references for several subsequent editions.

Two Nolo authors, Twila Slesnick, Ph.D, a tax and retirement specialist who provided clear answers on murky retirement plan issues; and Tony Mancuso, who provided up-to-the-minute information on small business law.

My colleagues and friends at Nolo, who make coming to work a genuine pleasure.

My family, who supply the love and support that makes everything else possible.

CONTENTS

CHAPTER 7

CREATE A LIVING TRUST

CHAPTER 8

TAKE ADVANTAGE OF SPECIAL PROCEDURES FOR SMALL ESTATES

CHAPTER 9

MAKE GIFTS

PUTTING IT ALL TOGETHER

GLOSSARY

INDEX

ICONS USED IN THIS BOOK

 CAUTION : Potential problem.

 FAST TRACK: Lets you know that you may be able to skip some material.

 RESOURCE: Refers you to another self-help resource.

 LAWYER: Situations when you should see a lawyer about a particular issue.

 TIP: A bit of advice that may help you with a particular issue.

INTRODUCTION

Thinking About Probate Avoidance

Probate, lawyers say, is simply a safeguard, designed to ensure that your wishes are honored and your family protected when you are no longer around to oversee matters yourself.

An impartial court supervises the whole process, to look out for the interests of both your family and your creditors. What's wrong with that?

A lot, unfortunately.

AN OVERVIEW OF PROBATE

During probate proceedings, a deceased person's will is brought to the local court. Proof must be shown that the will is authentic and was properly signed, with all the formalities required by state law. (If there is no valid will, the court determines who, under state law, stands to inherit the deceased's property.) The deceased person's property is inventoried and appraised, relatives and creditors are notified, and a notice is published in the local newspaper. Creditors make their claims, and debts are paid. Eventually—commonly, about a year later—the remaining property is distributed to the inheritors.

A. Why It's Worth Your While to Avoid Probate

Probate's problems have been well documented and well publicized. And if you've experienced the probate process firsthand, after the death of a parent or spouse, you probably don't need any convincing that avoidance is the best strategy. But in case you still aren't sure why planning to avoid probate is worth some effort, here is a summary of the important downsides.

Probate is a waste of money. The cost of probate varies widely from state to state, but probate attorney, court and other fees often eat up about 5% (or more) of the value of property left behind at death. As a result, that much less goes to the people or charities you wanted to get it. If the estate is complicated or disputed, the fees can be even larger.

TYPICAL PROBATE FEES

If you die with this much...	...probate may cost about this much
$200,000	$10,000
$400,000	$20,000

Probate's cost might be justified if the process really did something for families. But in most instances, there is no conflict, so there's no need to be in court.

For example, say a man leaves a will that gives everything to his widow and children, as is common. No one is challenging the validity of the will, and the family is perfectly willing to pay whatever bills he left and divide up the property according to his wishes. Why have a lengthy court proceeding, formal notification of relatives and creditors, and expensive publication of death notices in the "legal notices" column of a newspaper? The property merely needs to be handed over to the new owners, which is what probate-avoidance methods let you do. The successful use of living trusts and other probate avoidance techniques by millions of Americans is convincing evidence that if probate were gone, we wouldn't miss it.

Probate is a windfall for lawyers. Probate is such a profit center for lawyers that they go to great lengths to secure business (and to block legislative reforms that might render them superfluous). The probate windfall explains why lawyers usually charge so much less for wills than they do for other documents of comparable complexity: They are hoping to cash in later, when the will must be probated. It is no exaggeration to say that many lawyers plan for their later years by anticipating lucrative probate cases regularly coming their way.

A lawyer who accepts a probate case is almost guaranteed a nice profit for very little effort. Generally, probate entails lots of tedious paperwork but little or no original thinking. Most of the actual work is done by legal secretaries and paralegals. (In fact, more and more lawyers farm out the whole job—without telling the client—to form preparation services run by freelance paralegals.) There are few court appearances, if any, and very rarely is a lawyer called on to craft a legal argument or conduct anything resembling a trial.

Lawyers' fees, set by statute or local custom, often bear no relation to actual work done. Courts are supposed to keep an eye on fees, but in practice they very seldom intervene. And lawyers are almost always paid first—before the beneficiaries.

Some people slog through probate without hiring a lawyer, but in most states the system does nothing to encourage them. Just finding the right court can be a challenge. Depending on where you live, your will may be headed for Surrogate's Court, Orphans' Court, Circuit Court, Superior Court, or Chancery Court. Encouragingly, more probate courts are now putting at least some information on their websites. And in a few states, good self-help materials are available; for example, Nolo publishes *How to Probate an Estate in California*, by Julia Nissley.

Probate takes too long. Often, probate takes a year, during which time the beneficiaries generally get nothing unless the judge allows the immediate family a "family allowance." In some states, this allowance is a pittance, only a few hundred dollars. In others, it can amount to thousands. In any case, the family is forced to ask a court for use of its own money—a demeaning and absurd situation.

Delay can be more than an annoyance; it can cause major life disruptions. A student about to enter college may not be able to if a parent's assets are tied up in probate for months or years. A surviving spouse may not be able to move to take a new job. And it's especially hard to run—or sell—a small business with the court looking over your shoulder.

Probate is public. Few people ever stop to think that a will—a very personal document, which may reveal much about both financial and family circumstances—becomes a matter of public record after its writer dies. Like all other probate documents, wills are examined and filed, and can be inspected by anyone who goes to the courthouse and asks.

If you're rich or famous, you can count on public scrutiny. In any bookstore, you can find books of nothing but the wills of famous people; Jacqueline Kennedy Onassis's will popped up on the Internet almost instantly after it was filed in court. Obviously, precious few people generate the public interest of a Jackie O—but if you're well known in your community, reporters may sniff around just to see if there's anything they consider newsworthy. And con artists have been known to use public records to gather information about surviving family members who might be vulnerable to scams.

If, on the other hand, you arrange for your property to pass outside of probate—via a living trust or payable-on-death bank account, for example—the transaction is private. No documents are filed with a court or other government entity; what you leave to whom remains private. (There is one exception: Records of real estate ownership are always public.)

Each state requires a court proceeding. The only thing worse than regular probate is out-of-state probate. Usually, probate takes place in the county where the deceased person was living. But if there's real estate in another state, it's usually necessary to have a whole separate probate proceeding there, too. That means finding a lawyer in each state and financing multiple probate proceedings. No fun there.

WHY REFORM DOESN'T HAPPEN

If the probate system is such a mess, why hasn't it been cleaned up? It's the responsibility of state legislatures to change probate laws, and there have been some attempts at reform. But it's hardly a hot-button issue—no politician is going to get elected on a Probate Reform platform.

Some strides have been made, though. More than a dozen states have now adopted a set of laws called the Uniform Probate Code, which is aimed at simplifying the probate system. Probate in these states is generally much less of a hassle than regular probate in other states. And almost every state now has a streamlined probate procedure for "small estates." (See Chapter 8.)

Still, if the probate system were really gutted, it would threaten well-established interests. Probate lawyers, of course, stand to lose large amounts of easy money. Other industries milk the probate system as well: newspapers that publish the legal notices required in probate and businesses that sell the bonds executors must post, for example. Lobbyists for all these interests come out in force when proposed legislation would seriously cut into their profits.

The dearth of reform has, ultimately, spurred an end-run around probate. If you can't change it, people have decided, avoid it altogether.

B. What Probate Avoidance Can't Change

Avoiding probate has much to recommend it, as discussed above. But at the same time, it's not a magic bullet that solves every financial problem that might surface after your death. To clear up some common misconceptions, here are a few things that probate-avoidance has absolutely no effect on.

1. Taxes

Avoiding probate doesn't mean avoiding taxes. In fact, the two are completely unrelated. If you give away a lot of money during your life, or leave a lot at your death, the state and federal governments may take a chunk of it in the form of gift or estate tax. The government is uninterested in whether or not the property goes through probate court on its way to the people who inherit it.

Most people don't even need to think about federal gift and estate taxes. These taxes affect only people who make very large amounts of taxable gifts during life or leave very large estates at death. State taxes, however, may affect smaller estates. (Chapter 9 explains estate taxes.)

2. Your Family's Right to Inherit

If you're married, your spouse has a right to some of the property you leave at your death, and using probate-avoidance techniques to transfer the property doesn't change that. This, of course, is no problem for most people; most of us want very much to pass on to our spouses and children whatever wealth we've accumulated. In case you're concerned about this issue, however, here are the general rules regarding your family's rights:

Your spouse. Most married people leave much, if not all, of their property to their spouses. But if you don't, your spouse may have the right to go to court and claim some of your property after your death.

The rights of spouses vary from state to state. In the community property states (Arizona, California, Idaho, Louisiana, Nevada, New Mexico, Texas, Washington, and Wisconsin), the general rule is that spouses together own all property that either acquires during the marriage, except property one spouse receives by gift or inheritance. Each spouse owns a half-interest in this "community property." You are free to leave your separate property and your half of the community property to anyone you choose.

In all other states, a surviving spouse who doesn't receive at least one-third to one-half of the deceased spouse's property (through a will, living trust, or other method) is entitled to insist upon that much. The exact share depends on state law. In short, a spouse who doesn't receive the minimum he or she is entitled to under state law (the "statutory share") may be entitled to some of the property in your living trust.

Don't try to cut out your spouse. If you don't plan to leave at least half of the property in your estate to your spouse, you should consult a lawyer experienced in estate planning.

State law may also give your spouse the right to inherit the family residence, or at least use it for his or her life. The Florida constitution, for example, gives a surviving spouse the family residence. (Fla. Const. Art. 10, § 4.) The spouse is free, of course, to voluntarily give up this right.

More information. *Plan Your Estate,* by Denis Clifford and Cora Jordan (Nolo), contains a state-by-state list of surviving spouses' rights.

Children. Although most children inherit the bulk of their parents' property, usually after both parents have died, it isn't mandated by law. Put bluntly, you don't have to leave your children a dime.

The law protects only children who appear to have been accidentally overlooked—typically, children born after the parent's will is signed. Such children are entitled to a share (the size is determined by state law) of the deceased parent's estate, which may include property in a living trust.

So if you don't want to leave any property to one or more of your children—perhaps they already have plenty of money, or you've already given them their inheritances—just make a will and mention each child in it. And to avoid any later misunderstandings or hurt feelings, explain your actions to your children, either in your will or—better—now, in person.

Grandchildren have no right to inherit from their grandparents unless their parent has died. In that case, the grandchildren essentially take the place of the deceased child and are entitled to whatever he or she would have been legally entitled to, if anything.

3. Your Creditors' Rights

Avoiding probate doesn't let you off the hook from legal obligations to your creditors. If you don't leave enough other assets to pay your debts and taxes, any assets that passed outside of probate may be subject to the claims of creditors after your death.

If there is any probate proceeding, your executor (the person named in your will to handle your affairs after your death) can demand that whoever inherited the property turn over some or all of it so that creditors can be paid. Creditors, however, have only a set amount of time—about three to six months, in most states—to submit formal claims to your executor. A creditor who is properly notified of the probate court proceeding cannot file a claim after the deadline passes.

On the other hand, when property isn't probated, creditors' claims aren't cut off so quickly. In theory, at least, a creditor could track down the property and sue the new owner to collect the debt a year or two later.

Example: *Elaine is a real estate investor with a good-sized portfolio of property. At any one time she has many creditors, and she has even been sued once or twice. It might be to her advantage to have assets transferred by a probate court procedure, which requires creditors who are properly notified of the probate proceeding to file their claims promptly.*

As a practical matter, however, avoiding probate may actually provide more protection from creditors. When property is distributed without probate, there is no legal requirement (as there is in probate) that creditors be notified in writing. They may not know of the death for years. They may not know where the property went, and especially if the debt is small, it may not be worth their while to track down the new owners and try to collect.

Most people don't need to worry that after their death, creditors will line up to collect large debts from the estate. In most situations, the surviving relatives simply pay the valid debts, such as monthly bills, taxes, and medical and funeral expenses. But if you are concerned about the possibility of large claims, you may want to let your property go through probate.

⚠️ **It's all or nothing.** If you want to take advantage of probate's creditor cutoff, you must let all your property pass through probate. If not, the creditor could still sue (even after the probate claim deadline) and try to collect from the property that didn't go through probate.

C. Comparing Probate-Avoidance Methods

Given the plentiful drawbacks of probate, it's not surprising that people have sought ways around it. In a nutshell, you can avoid probate by using other documents in place of a will or by transferring property before your death.

Forty years ago, almost the only way to avoid probate was by using a trust. New methods have come along as part of new, government-created types of investments, such as private retirement accounts. People have eagerly taken up each new probate-avoidance method. In fact, "nonprobate transfers" have gotten so popular "that they now constitute a major, if not the major, form of wealth transmission," according to a committee of legal experts. (Intestacy, Wills, and Donative Transfers Act, 8B U.L.A. 3 (1993).)

This book discusses common and straightforward ways to avoid probate (And despite its title, it now discusses *nine* ways to avoid probate—a chapter on how to use transfer-on-death deeds was added when more and more states began allowing this important probate-avoidance method.). None of these methods requires hiring a lawyer; all involve very little or no expense.

Keep in mind that you can mix and match methods when you're planning to avoid probate. You may well want to use one technique for avoiding probate of real estate and another for stocks, for example. Some options for common kinds of assets are listed below. Not every option is available in every state; each method's advantages and limitations are discussed in detail later in the book.

CHOOSING THE RIGHT PROBATE-AVOIDANCE METHOD

Asset	What You Can Do to Avoid Probate
Real estate	Transfer to a living trust
	Hold property in joint tenancy with a co-owner or tenancy by the entirety with your spouse
	Hold as community property (or community property with right of survivorship) with your spouse
	Prepare a transfer-on-death deed
Bank accounts, certificates of deposit	Name a payable-on-death beneficiary
	Hold in joint tenancy with a co-owner or tenancy by the entirety with your spouse
	Hold as community property (or community property with right of survivorship) with your spouse
	Transfer to a living trust
Stocks and bonds	Name a transfer-on-death beneficiary
	Transfer to a living trust
	Hold in joint tenancy with a co-owner or tenancy by the entirety with your spouse
	Hold as community property (or community property with right of survivorship) with your spouse
Government bonds	Register ownership in beneficiary form
	Hold in joint tenancy with a co-owner or tenancy by the entirety with your spouse
	Hold as community property (or community property with right of survivorship) with your spouse
	Transfer to a living trust
Cars and other vehicles	Register in transfer-on-death form
	Hold in joint tenancy with a co-owner or tenancy by the entirety with your spouse
	Hold as community property (or community property with right of survivorship) with your spouse
	Transfer to a living trust
Retirement accounts (IRAs, 401(k) plans)	Name a beneficiary to inherit at your death

Not all of these probate-avoidance methods are available in every state, and not all are appropriate in every situation. The chapters on each method explain their restrictions, advantages, and disadvantages.

D. A Lick of Common Sense

Probate avoidance is not a religion—or at least, it shouldn't be. To hear some people, though (especially the ones selling various probate-avoidance advice or documents), failing to avoid probate for every one of your assets is tantamount to neglecting a moral duty to your family.

Don't believe it. Doing some planning so that your family will be spared red tape and expense after your death is sensible and laudable, but keep in mind that probate doesn't happen until after your death. There's just no reason for a healthy 40-year-old to spend lots of time and effort to avert something that probably won't happen for many, many years. If you're young and healthy, a will, which lets you leave property to the people you choose and name someone you want to raise your children if you can't, is probably all the estate planning you need; you can worry about probate later. And even if you never do a bit of probate-avoidance planning, your family will endure some hassle and expense— but will survive.

In other words, use common sense. As you get older and decide it's worthwhile to do some probate-avoidance planning, keep in mind that your family will reap the most benefits if your big-ticket possessions, like real estate and large bank or investment accounts, don't go through probate. So take advantage of the simple, inexpensive methods outlined in this book to remove those assets from the probate system. But don't get carried away with trying to get every last teaspoon covered by a sure-fire probate-avoidance method.

If you're determined to devote that much energy to what will happen after your death, far better to spend some of it on things that really matter: the memories you will leave with loved ones, the difference you will have made in others' lives. After all, would you really want as your epitaph, "Didn't Spend a Nickel on Probate Fees"?

■

Set Up Payable-on-Death Accounts

Payable-on-death bank accounts offer one of the easiest ways to keep money—even large sums of it—out of probate. All you need to do is properly notify your bank of whom you want to inherit the money in the account. The bank and the beneficiary you name will do the rest, bypassing probate court entirely. It's that simple.

This kind of account has been called the "poor man's trust." The description is apt (if sexist) because a payable-on-death account does accomplish for a bank account—for free—exactly the same result as would an expensive, lawyer-drawn trust.

As long as you are alive, the person you named to inherit the money in a payable-on-death (P.O.D.) account has no rights to it. If you need the money, or just change your mind about leaving it to the beneficiary you named, you can spend the money, name a different beneficiary, or close the account.

PAYABLE-ON-DEATH ACCOUNTS AT A GLANCE

Pros

- They're easy to create.
- There's no limit on how much money you can leave this way.
- Designating a beneficiary for a bank account costs nothing.
- It's easy for the beneficiary to claim the money after the original owner dies.

Cons

- You can't name an alternate beneficiary.

PAYABLE-ON-DEATH ACCOUNT OR "TOTTEN TRUST"?

Payable-on-death accounts go by different names in different states—and sometimes in the same state. Your bank, for example, may respond to your request for a payable-on-death account by handing you a form that authorizes the creation of something called a "Totten trust." Payable-on-death bank accounts are also sometimes called tentative trusts, informal trusts, or revocable bank account trusts.

"Totten trusts" are really just payable-on-death accounts. The name comes from an old New York case (*Re Totten*), which was the first case to rule (in 1904) that someone could open a bank account as "trustee" for another person who had no rights to the money until the depositor died. Other courts had balked at this, objecting that such an account was tantamount to a will, which had to fulfill detailed legal requirements to be valid. The Totten court called the account a "tentative" (revocable) trust.

After this decision, courts in many other states adopted the idea of Totten trusts. Later, state legislatures enacted statutes authorizing payable-on-death accounts, specifically addressing many of the questions that had sprung up about Totten trusts. For example, some statutes state exactly how you can change a payable-on-death designation.

A. The Paperwork

Banks, savings and loans, and credit unions all offer payable-on-death accounts. They don't charge any extra fees for keeping your money this way. You can add a payable-on-death designation to any kind of new or existing account: checking, savings, or certificate of deposit.

Setting up a payable-on-death bank account is simple. When you open the account and fill out the bank's forms, just list the beneficiary on the signature card. The bank may also ask you for some other information, such as the beneficiary's address and birth date. (For example, the current address of each beneficiary is required by law in a few states.) The beneficiary of a payable-on-death account, who is commonly referred to as a "P.O.D. payee," doesn't have to sign anything.

Example: *Magda wants to leave her two nieces some money. She opens a savings account at a local bank, deposits $10,000 in it, and names her two nieces as payable-on-death beneficiaries. After Magda's death ten years later, they claim the money in the account—including the interest paid by the bank—without going through probate.*

If you choose an account that has restrictions on withdrawals—for example, a 24-month certificate of deposit—the early withdrawal penalty will probably be waived if you die before the period is up.

If you've considered changing a solely owned bank account to a joint account with the person you want to inherit the money after your death, you may be better off by simply naming the person as the P.O.D. beneficiary instead. There are several advantages.

If you added another person's name to yours on the account, he or she would immediately have the right to withdraw money from the account. And if she got behind on her debts, a creditor could come after her share of the account. (See Chapter 6.)

Example: *Matthew, an elderly widower, goes down to his bank and makes his daughter, Doris, the payable-on-death beneficiary of his checking account. Doris (and her creditors) will have no access to the money during Matthew's life, but after his death she'll be able to get the funds in the account quickly and easily.*

⚠️ **Don't create a joint account just to avoid probate.** If you want to leave money to someone at your death—but not give it away now—stick to a P.O.D. account. It will accomplish your goal simply and easily. Don't set up a joint account with the understanding that the other person will withdraw money only after you die. This is a common mistake, and it often creates confusion and family fights.

B. Adding a P.O.D. Designation to a Joint Account

P.O.D. accounts can be very useful for couples who have joint bank accounts.

1. Accounts With a Right of Survivorship

Most joint accounts come with what's called the "right of survivorship," meaning that when one co-owner dies, the other will automatically be the sole owner of the account. So when the first owner dies, the funds in the account belong to the survivor—without probate. If you add a P.O.D. designation, it takes effect only when the second owner dies. Then, whatever is in the account goes to the P.O.D. beneficiary you named.

Example: *Virginia and Percy keep a joint checking account with several thousand dollars in it. They hold this account as joint tenants with right of survivorship. They decide to name their sons, who are both adults, as P.O.D. beneficiaries. After both Virginia and Percy have died, the bank will release whatever is left in the account to the sons, in equal shares.*

It's important for both spouses (or other co-owners) to realize that designating a P.O.D. beneficiary for a joint account doesn't lock in the surviving spouse after one spouse dies. The survivor is free to change the beneficiary or close the account, shutting out the beneficiary who was named back when both spouses were still alive.

Example: *Howard and Marge name Elaine, Howard's daughter from a previous marriage, as the P.O.D. payee of their joint savings account. Howard dies first, and in the years that follow relations between Marge and Elaine deteriorate. Marge decides to remove Elaine as P.O.D. beneficiary and instead name her nephew, Max. When Marge dies, Elaine doesn't inherit any of the money in the account—even though she's firmly convinced that her father intended her to.*

Adding a P.O.D. beneficiary to a joint account not only avoids probate, but allows you to plan for the unlikely event that both persons die simultaneously.

Example: *June and Horace have a joint savings account. They name their daughter, Virginia, as the payable-on-death beneficiary. When June and Horace are killed in an accident, Virginia inherits the money in the account without probate.*

2. Accounts With No Right of Survivorship

Some kinds of joint accounts cannot be turned into payable-on-death accounts. Unless your joint account provides that when one owner dies, the other automatically becomes the sole owner, don't try to name a P.O.D. payee for the account.

Two common situations where this advice applies are:

• Your state law requires you to request the right of survivorship in writing when you open the account, and you didn't make the proper request. In that case, the account is not a joint tenancy account; it's what is known as a "tenancy in common" account, which means that you can leave your share to anyone you choose.

• You and your spouse live in a community property state and own a community property account together. Such accounts don't carry the right of survivorship; each spouse has the right to leave his or her half-interest to someone else.

⚠ **Don't use a P.O.D. designation for a joint account that doesn't have the right of survivorship.** In other words, don't try to arrange things so that a P.O.D. payee inherits just your share of a co-owned bank account at your death. It's far more reliable and less confusing to establish a separate account and name a P.O.D. payee for it.

C. Choosing Beneficiaries

There are few restrictions on whom you can name as a P.O.D. beneficiary. But there are some issues you should think about as you make
your choices.

EXTRA FDIC COVERAGE FOR MOST BENEFICIARIES

Payable-on-death accounts get extra coverage from the Federal
Deposit Insurance Corporation, in some cases. It depends on whom the
beneficiaries are.

The general rule is that the FDIC insures each person's accounts at a
financial institution up to $100,000. But with a P.O.D. account, each
beneficiary's interest in the account is insured for up to $100,000—if
the beneficiary is a close relative of the account owner. To get this extra
protection, the beneficiary must be a spouse, child, grandchild, parent,
or sibling.

For example, if you have a $300,000 account and name your
spouse and your son as P.O.D. beneficiaries, $200,000 is covered by
FDIC insurance. Your spouse and son are entitled to $100,000 each in
coverage.

To check on FDIC coverage for your accounts, use the "Electronic
Deposit Insurance Estimator" at www.fdic.gov.

1. Children

It's perfectly fine to name a minor—that is, a child younger than 18
years old—as a P.O.D. payee. If the account is worth more than a few
thousand dollars, however, you should think about what might happen
if that beneficiary were still a child at your death. You will probably
want to arrange for an adult to manage the money for the child.

If you don't, and a minor child inherits money from a payable-on-
death account, one of three things will happen:

- If state law allows it, the money, no matter how much, can simply be given to the beneficiary's parents (or to the beneficiary, if he or she is married). The parents hold the money for the benefit of the child.

- If the amount is relatively small—generally, a few thousand dollars, depending on state law and bank custom—the bank will probably turn it over to the child or the child's parents.

- If the amount is larger, the parents will probably have to go to court and ask to be appointed guardians of the money. (If the parents aren't alive, a guardian will probably already have been appointed and supervised by the court.)

Fortunately, court involvement, which can be expensive, intrusive, and time-consuming, can be easily avoided. You can choose someone, now, and give that person authority to manage the money, without court supervision, in case the child is still younger than 18 at your death. The logical choice, usually, is one of the child's parents.

The easiest way to do this, in most states, is to name an adult to serve as "custodian" of the money. Custodians are authorized under a law called the Uniform Transfers to Minors Act (UTMA), which has been adopted by every state except South Carolina and Vermont.

All you need to do is name the custodian as the P.O.D. payee of the account and make it clear that the custodian is to act on the child's behalf. That gives the custodian the legal responsibility to manage and use the money for the benefit of the child. Then, when the child reaches adulthood, the custodian turns over what's left to the beneficiary. Most, but not all, UTMA states set 21 as the age when the custodianship ends. (The ages are listed below.)

AGE AT WHICH AN UTMA CUSTODIANSHIP ENDS

Alabama	21	Missouri	21
Alaska	18 to 25*	Montana	21
Arizona	21	Nebraska	21
Arkansas	18 to 21*	Nevada	18 to 25*
California	18 to 25*	New Hampshire	21
Colorado	21	New Jersey	18 to 21*
Connecticut	21	New Mexico	21
Delaware	21	New York	21
District of Columbia	18 to 21*	North Carolina	18 to 21*
Florida	21	North Dakota	21
Georgia	21	Ohio	21
Hawaii	21	Oklahoma	18 to 21*
Idaho	21	Oregon	21 to 25*
Illinois	21	Pennsylvania	21 to 25*
Indiana	21	Rhode Island	21
Iowa	21	South Dakota	18
Kansas	21	Tennessee	21 to 25*
Kentucky	18	Texas	21
Louisiana	18	Utah	21
Maine	18 to 21*	Virginia	18 to 21*
Maryland	21	Washington	21
Massachusetts	21	West Virginia	21
Michigan	18 to 21*	Wisconsin	21
Minnesota	21	Wyoming	21
Mississippi	21		

*The person who sets up the custodianship can designate the age, within these limits, at which the custodianship ends and the beneficiary inherits the money outright.

Example: *Alice wants to make her grandson, Tyler, the P.O.D. payee of a bank account. But Tyler is just 9 years old. So Alice decides to name Tyler's mother, Susan, as custodian of the money in the account. On the bank's form, Alice puts, in the space for the P.O.D. payee, "Susan Irving, as custodian for Tyler Irving under the Florida Uniform Transfers to Minors Act." If Tyler is not yet 21 when his grandmother dies, Susan will be legally in charge of the money until Tyler's 21st birthday.*

IF YOU DON'T LIVE IN AN UTMA STATE

Even if you live in a state that has not adopted the UTMA, you may still be able to enjoy the law's benefits. The law is written so that you can appoint a custodian if any of the following is true:

- The custodian lives in a state that has adopted the law.
- The minor lives in a state that has adopted the law.
- The bank account (the "custodial property," in the terms of the statute) is located in a state that has adopted the law.

Example 1: *Christopher is a resident of South Carolina, which has not adopted the UTMA. His grandson, however, lives in California, which has. Christopher can appoint a custodian for his grandson under the California Uniform Transfers to Minors Act. As long as the boy is a resident of California when the transfer takes place, the transfer is valid under the UTMA.*

Example 2: *Eunice, a Vermonter, keeps an account in a New Hampshire bank. She can use the New Hampshire UTMA to appoint a custodian for her granddaughter. On the bank forms, she can name "Esther Stanhope, as custodian for Michelle Stanhope under the New Hampshire Uniform Transfers to Minors Act."*

2. Multiple Beneficiaries

You may well want to name more than one person to inherit the money in a bank account—for example, your three children or two good friends. That's no problem; you just name all the beneficiaries on the bank's form. Each will inherit an equal share of the money in the account unless you specify otherwise.

> **Be careful when setting up unequal shares.** In a few states—Florida, for example—you cannot change the equal-shares rule. If you're concerned about this issue, check your state's law or open a separate account for each beneficiary.

It's important to realize that you can't name an alternate payee—that is, someone to inherit the money if your first choice doesn't outlive you. In other words, if you list three payees on a bank's form, the bank won't consider your list to be a ranking in order of preference. For example, some bank forms provide three spaces for beneficiaries' names. It's not uncommon for people to assume that beneficiary #1 will get all the money, and that if he isn't alive at your death, then #2 will inherit it, and so on. But that's not the way it works. All the beneficiaries you name will share the money in the account.

If one of the beneficiaries dies before you do, all the money will go to the surviving beneficiaries. So if you leave an account to your three children, and one of them dies before you do, the other two will inherit the funds. Depending on your family situation, this result may be fine with you—or it may not. If it's not what you want, you should name new P.O.D. payees after a beneficiary dies.

Example: *Miranda names her sons, Brad and Eric, as P.O.D. beneficiaries of her bank account. Eric dies before Miranda does, leaving two children of his own. Unless Miranda changes her bank account papers to include the grandchildren as P.O.D. beneficiaries, they will not inherit their father's share. Instead, all the money in the account will belong to Brad when Miranda dies.*

3. Institutions

It's unlikely, but your state's law may restrict your ability to name an institution, such as a school, church, or other charity, as the beneficiary of a P.O.D. account. Delaware law, for example, requires the beneficiary to be "a natural person."

Such a requirement can frustrate attempts to leave money as you wish. In 1981, for example, an Ohio court invalidated a payable-on-death designation on a certificate of deposit that named a church as the beneficiary. The court ruled that state law required a P.O.D. beneficiary to be a "natural person," not a corporation. (*Powell v. City Nat. Bank & Trust Co.*, 2 Ohio App. 3d 1, 2 Ohio BR 1, 440 N.E.2d 560 (1981).) After this decision, the Ohio legislature changed the law to allow any entity or organization to be a P.O.D. beneficiary.

4. Your Spouse's Rights

You may not have complete freedom to dispose of the funds in a bank account—even if it's in your name—as you wish. Your spouse (or in a few states, your registered domestic partner) may have rights, too. It depends on your state's law.

COMMUNITY PROPERTY STATES		NON-COMMUNITY PROPERTY STATES
Alaska*	Nevada	All other states
Arizona	New Mexico	
California	Texas	
Idaho	Washington	
Louisiana	Wisconsin	

*Only if spouses sign a community property agreement.

⚠️ **You can't shortchange creditors or family.** If you don't leave enough other assets to pay your debts and taxes or to support your spouse and minor children temporarily, a P.O.D. bank account may be subject to the claims of creditors or your family after your death. If there is any probate proceeding, your executor can demand that a P.O.D. beneficiary turn over some or all of the funds so that creditors can be paid.

If you specifically pledged the account as collateral for a debt, the creditor is entitled to (and doubtless will) claim repayment directly from the funds in the account. The P.O.D. payee gets whatever, if anything, is left.

a. Spouses' Rights in Community Property States

If you live in a community property state, your spouse (or in California, your registered domestic partner) probably already owns half of whatever you have in a bank account, even if the account is in your name only. If you contributed money you earned while married, that money and the interest earned on it is "community property," and your spouse is legally entitled to half.

There are a few exceptions to this rule: Your money is yours to do with as you please if you and your spouse have signed a valid agreement to keep all your property separate. And your spouse does not have any right to your separate property—money you deposited before you were married, or money that you alone inherited or received as a gift—unless that money has been mixed with community property in a bank account and is impossible to separate.

If the money in your account is community property, and you want to name someone other than your spouse as the P.O.D. beneficiary for the whole account, it's a good idea to get your spouse's written consent.

Otherwise, your spouse could assert a claim to half of the money in the account at your death, leaving the beneficiary you named with only half.

b. Spouses' Rights in Non-Community Property States

If you leave money in a P.O.D. bank account to someone other than your spouse, make sure your spouse doesn't object to your overall estate plan.

In non-community property states (all states except the ones listed above), surviving spouses who are unhappy with what the deceased spouse left them can claim a certain percentage of the deceased spouse's property. This is called the spouse's "elective share" or "statutory share," and in most states it amounts to about a third of what the spouse owned. It's a fairly rare occurrence, however, for a spouse to go to court over this, because most spouses inherit more than their statutory share.

The funds in a P.O.D. account may be subject to a spouse's claim— or they may not, depending on state law. Some states consider such accounts outside the surviving spouse's reach.

CONTRACTUAL WILLS

It's an infrequent practice these days, but some couples make legally binding agreements to leave property to each other. They sign a contract that requires them in turn to sign wills leaving all their assets (or part of them) to each other. These contracts have been ruled to take precedence over a payable-on-death designation on a bank account. In other words, the P.O.D. designation gets wiped out by the contract.

Example: *Scott and Terry sign a contract in which each promises to make a will leaving all their assets to the other. Later, Scott adds a payable-on-death designation to his savings account, naming his brother as the beneficiary. If Scott dies first, Terry has a legal right to the funds in the account.*

D. If a Beneficiary Dies Before You Do

People usually choose people younger than themselves to inherit their money and property, fully expecting them to outlive their elders. But sometimes this natural course of events is disrupted. If someone you have named as a P.O.D. beneficiary dies before you do, you should change the necessary paperwork at the bank to put a new beneficiary in place.

If you named more than one payee, and one or more of them dies before you do, the funds in the account will go to the survivor(s) at your death. (See Section C, above.)

If, however, none of the P.O.D. payees you named is alive at your death, the bank will release the funds in the account to your executor, who will be responsible for seeing that the money is distributed under the terms of your will or state law. The money will probably have to go through probate, unless your estate is small enough to qualify for special, simpler procedures. (Chapter 8 discusses these probate short-cuts.)

If you want to name alternate beneficiaries, don't rely on a P.O.D. account. Banks generally don't allow you to name an alternate P.O.D. payee—that is, someone who would inherit the money if none of your primary beneficiaries outlived you.

Your will, if you make one (and you should, for reasons like this) functions as a backup in this case, as explained below. But that doesn't avoid probate. If you want to name a back-up beneficiary and be sure of avoiding probate, you'll probably want to use a living trust. (See Chapter 7.)

Depending on state law, however, the bank may be able to release the money directly to your legal heirs—the close relatives who are entitled to inherit from you if you don't leave a will. In that case, the money won't have to go through probate.

If the money goes to your executor, it will be distributed under the terms of your will, even though you most likely didn't even mention this account in your will. That's because most wills contain what is called a "residuary clause," which names a beneficiary to inherit everything that's not specifically mentioned in the will. The person you named to inherit this "residuary" property would receive this money.

Example: *Mark names his brother as the P.O.D. beneficiary of his savings account. But his brother dies, and Mark, confined to a nursing home, isn't able to change the paperwork at the bank to name a new payee. Mark does, however, have a will that contains a residuary clause, naming his daughter Madeline as residuary beneficiary. When Mark dies, and the will is probated, the money in the account goes to her, along with everything else that Mark didn't specifically leave to another beneficiary.*

E. If You Change Your Mind

Families change; relationships change. At some point you may decide that you don't want to leave money to a P.O.D. payee you've named, or a beneficiary may die before you do. You're free to change the P.O.D. arrangement, but you must meticulously follow the procedures for making changes. The law books, sadly, are full of cases brought by relatives fighting over the bank accounts of their deceased loved ones who didn't pay enough attention to these simple rules.

1. How to Change a P.O.D. Designation

There are two easy and foolproof ways to make a change to a P.O.D. account:

- Withdraw the money in the account, or
- Go to the bank and change the paperwork. Fill out, sign, and deliver to the bank a new account registration card that names a different beneficiary or removes the P.O.D. designation altogether.

To ensure that your wishes are followed after your death, dot the i's and cross the t's when it comes to following the bank's procedures. A change in beneficiary isn't effective unless you fulfill the bank's requirements, whatever they are. Almost all banks require something in writing—a phone call isn't good enough. And to be effective, in most places your written instructions must be received by the bank before your death.

That doesn't sound difficult, but it's not all that unusual to find problems. In one case, after a woman's death a new signature card, in a stamped envelope, was found on her desk. Relatives sued over the money. The court ruled that the change was not effective because the new signature card was ambiguous and because the bank had not received it before her death. (*Codispoti v. Mid-America Federal Savings and Loan Ass'n*, No. 85AP-451, Ohio App. 1986.)

2. Contradictory Will Provisions

Trying to change a P.O.D. designation in your will, by leaving the account to someone else, is almost certain to cause problems after your death. At best, it will spawn confusion; at worst, disagreements or even a lawsuit.

About half the states say, flat out, that a P.O.D. designation cannot be overridden or changed in a will. In these states, a will provision that purports to name a new beneficiary for a P.O.D. account will simply have no effect.

Example: *Kimberly names her niece, Patricia, as the P.O.D. beneficiary of her bank account. After they have a falling-out, Kimberly writes her will, and in it leaves the funds in the account to her friend Charles. At Kimberly's death, Patricia is still legally entitled to collect the money.*

Some other states do allow you to revoke a payable-on-death designation in your will if you specifically identify the account and the beneficiary. An attempt to wipe out several accounts with a general statement won't work. In one case, a South Dakota woman wrote in her will that "I hereby intentionally revoke any joint tenancies or trust arrangements commonly called 'Totten trusts' [another name for P.O.D. accounts] by this will." After her death, a court ruled that even this language wasn't specific enough; state law requires every P.O.D. account to be individually changed or revoked. (*In re Estate of Sneed*, 521 N.W.2d 675 (S. Dak. 1994).)

The moral: **Never rely on your will to change a payable-on-death account**. Instead, deal directly with the bank, which, after all, will be in charge of the money after your death.

3. Property Settlement Agreements at Divorce

A property settlement agreement, even though it's approved by a court when a couple divorces, may not revoke a payable-on-death designation.

For example, when a New York couple divorced, the property settlement agreement gave the husband "any and all bank accounts, held jointly or otherwise." Some of those accounts named the wife as payable-on-death beneficiary; when the husband died, she inherited the money. The court ruled that because the settlement agreement had not named the accounts specifically, it had not met New York's statutory requirements for the revocation of a Totten trust account. (*Eredics v. Chase Manhattan Bank, N.A.*, 760 N.Y.S.2d 737 (Ct. App. 2003).)

Similarly, when an Arizona couple divorced, their property settlement agreement gave the husband some bank CDs for which he had named the wife as the payable-on-death payee. But the husband never went to the bank and removed the wife as the P.O.D. payee. When he died, a court ruled that the ex-wife was entitled to the money, because the settlement agreement had no effect on the contract between the husband and the bank. (*Jordan v. Burgbacher,* 883 P.2d 458 (Ariz. Ct. App. 1994).)

F. Claiming the Money

After your death, all a P.O.D. beneficiary needs to do to claim the money is show the bank a certified copy of the death certificate and proof of his or her identity. If the account was a joint account to begin with, the bank will need to see the death certificates of all the original owners. The bank records will show that the beneficiary is entitled to whatever money is in the account.

State laws authorize banks to release the money in payable-on-death accounts when they're shown this proof of the account holder's death; they don't need probate court approval. Legally, the money automatically belongs to the beneficiaries when the original account owner dies. It's not under the control of the probate court.

Beneficiaries may, however, encounter some delays when they go to claim the money:

- **Tax clearances.** Like other bank accounts, a payable-on-death account may be temporarily frozen at your death, if your state levies death taxes. The bank will release the money to your beneficiaries when the state is satisfied that your estate has ample funds to pay the taxes.

- **Waiting periods.** There may be a short waiting period before the money can be claimed. Vermont, for example, doesn't allow a bank to release funds to P.O.D. beneficiaries until 90 days after the death of the account owner.

When you set up a P.O.D. account, ask the bank what the P.O.D. payee will need to do to claim the money after your death. Then make sure the payee knows what to expect.

■

CHAPTER 2

Name a Beneficiary for Your Retirement Accounts

Millions of employees and small business owners are now in charge of their own retirement plans. They are setting up and keeping an eye on their Individual Retirement Accounts (IRAs) or Keoghs, or contributing to 401(k) plans (or 403(b) plans, for employees of non-profit organizations or public schools) under programs set up by their employers. More than half a trillion dollars has already been invested in 401(k) plans alone, according to one estimate.

These accounts offer tax breaks that will let your savings grow quickly, providing retirement income later. And even after your death, they can give more benefits for your family because they avoid probate, too. Any money left in one of these accounts at your death goes to the beneficiaries you chose—without going through probate.

When a beneficiary withdraws the money from a 401(k) plan or traditional IRA after your death, the tax deferral ends; the money is treated as taxable income of the beneficiary. This is unlike other inherited assets, which are not subject to income tax. Money withdrawn from a Roth IRA, however, generally is not taxed.

The IRS publishes thick books containing nothing but retirement plan rules. These regulations are often next to impossible to figure out, and of course they can change at any time. This chapter focuses on the relatively simple task of choosing a beneficiary to inherit the money without probate. It also touches on some important IRS rules about required withdrawals from the two most common types of retirement plans, IRAs and 401(k) plans.

THE TAX ADVANTAGES OF RETIREMENT PLANS

Traditional IRAs and 401(k) Plans. First, the money you deposit each year (up to the legal limit, which depends on the type of retirement plan) is tax-deductible. That means at income tax time, you can reduce your taxable income by the amount of your contribution.

Second, the income and profits that come from investing the money you save generally aren't taxed now, either. All of it can be reinvested and start earning income itself.

Of course, nothing good lasts forever. Eventually, you must start making withdrawals, and when you do, the money you take out will be subject to income tax (unless some of your contributions were not tax-deductible). By then, however, presumably you'll be retired and in a lower tax bracket. (Internal Rev. Code §§ 72, 219.)

Roth IRAs. The Roth IRA is a whole different animal. Contributions are not tax-deductible. Income accumulates tax-free, however, as long as the contributions stay in the account at least five years. Most important, qualified withdrawals are not taxed. There are no mandatory lifetime withdrawals.

A. Choosing a Beneficiary

When you create an IRA or enroll in a 401(k) plan, the forms you fill out will ask you to name a beneficiary. You will probably also be given the opportunity to name an alternate (sometimes called "secondary" or "contingent") beneficiary, who will inherit the money if your first choice dies before you do or at the same time.

Choosing who will inherit the funds in your retirement account is, obviously, a very important decision. If you're single, you're free to choose whomever you want as the beneficiary. If you're married, how-ever, the law may restrict your choices significantly.

NAMING A RETIREMENT ACCOUNT BENEFICIARY AT A GLANCE

Pros

- Easy and free to set up.
- You can change your mind and name a different bene-ficiary at any time (subject to certain rights of your spouse).
- It's easy for the beneficiary to claim the money after your death.

Cons

- Your retirement plan may not allow you to name an alternate beneficiary.
- Federal law requires mandatory withdrawals from traditional IRAs and from 401(k) accounts.

---

1. Special Rules If You're Married or Divorced

Most married people choose their spouses to inherit the money in a retirement account. It's often a good choice for financial reasons as well as personal ones, as discussed below (see Section 2).

If you want to name a different beneficiary, you may run into complications from several state and federal laws, intended to make sure your spouse isn't left out in the cold if you die first. Their effect depends on the kind of retirement account you have and where you live.

⚠️ **Get your spouse's consent in writing.** No matter what kind of retirement account you have, it's always a good idea—and may be required by law, as discussed below—to get your spouse's written consent before naming someone else as beneficiary.

a. 401(k) Plans

A special rule applies to 401(k) plans (and other "qualified plans"): Your spouse is entitled to inherit all the money in the account *unless* he or she signs a written waiver, consenting to your choice of another beneficiary. It's not enough just to name someone else on the beneficiary form that your employer gives you.

Especially if your spouse will be well provided for from other sources, the two of you may decide it makes sense to leave the money to someone else. If your spouse agrees to sign the waiver, which should be provided by the firm that administers the 401(k) plan, a plan representative or a notary public must act as a witness. A prenuptial agreement can't take the place of a waiver; the law says the *spouse* (not soon-to-be-spouse) must sign. A spouse who does sign a waiver can withdraw that consent if the other spouse later names a different beneficiary, unless the signing spouse expressly gave up that right. (IRC § 417(a)(2).)

Divorce. If you name your spouse as beneficiary of a 401(k) plan, pension plan, or employer-provided life insurance policy, and later divorce, a number of states have laws that automatically revoke your ex-spouse's right to inherit. These laws are no longer valid, under a ruling made by the U.S. Supreme Court. (*Egelhoff v. Egelhoff*, 532 U.S. 141 (2001).)

The Court's decision was based on the fact that 401(k) and similar plans, including severance plans and employee savings accounts, are governed by a federal law, the Employee Retirement Income Security Act (ERISA). That law, the Court ruled, requires the plan administrator to simply pay the proceeds to the beneficiary named by the plan participant—not to figure out who should get them under a particular state's law.

b. Individual Retirement Accounts

If you don't live in a community property state (listed below), you are free to name whomever you wish as your IRA beneficiary, even if you're married.

If, however, you live in a community property state, read on. Chances are your spouse owns half of what you have socked away in a retirement account. If any of the money you contributed was earned while you were married, that money remains "community property," and your spouse owns half.

 Domestic partners. California is the only state that allows registered domestic partners to own community property.

COMMUNITY PROPERTY STATES

Alaska*	Nevada
Arizona	New Mexico
California	Texas
Idaho	Washington
Louisiana	Wisconsin

*Only if spouses sign a community property agreement.

There are a few exceptions to this rule: Your spouse does not have any right to money you contributed before you were married or money that you alone inherited or were given. And the money you earned is yours to do with as you please if you and your spouse signed a valid agreement to keep all your property separate.

If the money in your retirement account is community property, and you want to name someone other than your spouse as the beneficiary, get your spouse's consent in writing. Some retirement plans, in fact, won't let you name someone else without this consent. If your spouse doesn't consent, the beneficiary you name will be entitled to only half of what's in the retirement account at your death.

State law may set out the rules about your spouse's consent. For example, in California, the spouse's consent must be in writing. The spouse can revoke the consent, again in writing, anytime before your death—in a will, for example. To be effective, the revocation must be delivered to you in a manner set out by the statute. (Cal. Prob. Code § 2031.)

2. Naming Your Spouse

If, like the great majority of married people, you want to name your husband or wife to inherit your retirement savings, you're making a good choice. A surviving spouse who is the sole beneficiary has more flexibility about what to do with the money than do other beneficiaries. Unlike other beneficiaries, who must start to withdraw the money in the year after your death (though not necessarily all at once, as discussed below), a surviving spouse, in some cases, can keep *all* the money tax-deferred at least for a while. (This isn't a concern with the Roth IRA, because withdrawals generally aren't taxed.)

A surviving spouse has three options. They are basically the same whether the account owner dies before or after reaching the age at which required minimum withdrawals (discussed in Section B, below) must begin. There is, however, one significant exception: If the minimum withdrawals have become necessary, then the surviving spouse must make the withdrawal for the year of death. After that, he or she can exercise one of the following choices.

a. Roll Over the Account

A spouse who is the sole beneficiary can "roll over" the money in the retirement account (IRA or qualified plan such as a 401(k)) to her own IRA. To do that, the spouse needs to contact the retirement account administrator and complete some paperwork.

Once the account has been rolled over, everything is just as if the surviving spouse were the original owner. The surviving spouse can name a beneficiary to inherit the funds at her death. Required minimum distributions will begin when she reaches 70½, and the amounts will be based on her life expectancy as set out in IRS tables. (Or, if the spouse remarries, required withdrawals will be based on the joint life expectancy of the survivor and the new spouse.)

The surviving spouse doesn't have to pay income tax on money in the account until it is withdrawn. Meanwhile, the funds can keep earning tax-deferred income.

A rollover can happen at any time—the survivor could do it years after the spouse's death. There's rarely a reason to wait. It might make sense, however, if the survivor is under age 59½ and wants to withdraw money from the account. Beneficiaries are not subject to the usual 10% "early distribution" (before age 59½) penalty, but they lose that special exemption if they roll over the account.

Example: *Annie is 45, with two children still at home, when her husband dies and she inherits the money in his 401(k) plan account. She may need to withdraw money from the account in the next few years.*

If she rolled over the money into her own retirement account, and then withdrew some of it before age 59½, she would have to pay the 10% early withdrawal penalty. So instead, she leaves the money in her late husband's account. It will continue to earn income that won't be taxed until she withdraws it, and she can make withdrawals without penalty.

b. Leave the Account in the Deceased Spouse's Name

A spouse who is the sole beneficiary can leave the retirement account in the deceased spouse's name. The survivor must begin taking required distributions by the later of:

- December 31 of the year after the deceased spouse's death, or
- the year the deceased spouse would have turned 70½.

The survivor can name a beneficiary, but the amount of the minimum required distributions is determined by the surviving spouse's life expectancy, as found in the IRS single life expectancy table. She can't use the Uniform table that assumes a beneficiary who is ten years younger.

c. Treat the Account as Her Own (IRAs only)

Even without a formal rollover, the surviving spouse can change an IRA (but not a 401(k) or other qualified plan) into her own if she:

- doesn't take a required distribution when it's supposed to be taken, or
- makes additional contributions to the IRA.

If the surviving spouse does either of these things, it's just as if she had rolled over the IRA into her own name. If the spouse does want to roll over an IRA, however, it's better to follow the formal rollover procedures—that way, there will be clear records of what was done.

Your surviving spouse may need professional advice. When your beneficiary eventually inherits the money in your retirement account—which, of course, might be many years down the line—he or she may want to get advice from a knowledgeable tax, investment, or pension specialist. IRS rules change, as do investment strategies, and your beneficiary will want to know the pros and cons of all options available under the current law.

3. Naming an Adult Other Than Your Spouse

Subject to your spouse's rights (this very important restriction is discussed above), you can name whomever you want to inherit your qualified plan or IRA account.

If you name two or more persons as beneficiaries, they will get equal shares unless you specify otherwise in the documents that set up the account.

After your death, the beneficiary gets whatever money is left in your retirement account. Simple, right? Well, not exactly. It's true that the beneficiary can, almost immediately, take out the money. But it's common for a beneficiary to prefer to keep at least some of the money in the account, where it can continue to earn tax-deferred income. Your beneficiary's choices depend on how old you are when you die.

If you die before you are required to take minimum distributions from your account (see Section B, below). IRS rules now allow the beneficiary you named (your spouse or someone else) to withdraw the money in your account over his or her own life expectancy.

If the beneficiary doesn't need all the money right away, spreading out the withdrawals offers several advantages. Obviously, it lets the beneficiary postpone paying the income tax that is due when money is withdrawn. And if the money were taken in a lump sum over just a few years, it might bump the recipient into a higher tax bracket.

If you die after required minimum distributions have begun. In the year of death, the beneficiary you named must withdraw as much as you would have been required to. After that, minimum distributions are based on the life expectancy of your beneficiary. That person looks up his or her life expectancy (from an IRS table) and then subtracts one every year.

For a Roth IRA, which has no mandatory lifetime withdrawals, the options for beneficiaries remain the same as if the death had occurred before required minimum withdrawals had begun.

4. Naming Minor Children

You can name a minor—that is, a child younger than 18 years old—as the beneficiary of your retirement account. In fact, children are common beneficiaries; single parents may name their own children, and grandparents may wish to leave some money directly to grandchildren. Or you may have a favorite young relative or friend you'd like to help out. And even if you don't name a child as your primary beneficiary, you may well want to name one as an alternate.

There is, however, a potential problem. If that beneficiary is still a minor at your death, you will want to arrange for an adult to manage the money.

If you don't make some arrangements, and a child inherits more than a few thousand dollars, the child's parents, if they're alive, will probably have to go to court and ask to be appointed guardians of the money. If neither parent is alive, the child's court-appointed and court-supervised guardian will handle the child's money.

Fortunately, this layer of court involvement, which can be expensive, intrusive, and time-consuming, can be easily avoided. You can choose someone now and give that person authority to manage the money without court supervision, in case the beneficiary inherits the money while still a minor. The logical choice, usually, is one of the child's parents.

The easiest way to do this, if your state law allows it, is to name an adult to serve as "custodian" of the money. Custodians are authorized under a law called the Uniform Transfers to Minors Act (UTMA), which has been adopted by all but a few states. The UTMA is explained in detail in Chapter 1, Section C.

5. Naming More Than One Beneficiary

It's generally a bad idea to name more than one beneficiary. There are a couple of reasons.

First, if you name your spouse and someone else as co-beneficiaries, your spouse loses the special benefits and flexibility she would otherwise have (see Section 2, above).

Second, it complicates things. If you die before age 70½, then multiple beneficiaries can split your account, and each can use his or her own life expectancy to determine the minimum amount they must withdraw each year. But if your beneficiaries inherit after you reached age 70½ and had to begin making minimum withdrawals (discussed in Section B, below), the total amount that must be withdrawn each year is based on the statistical life expectancy of the oldest beneficiary. If some beneficiaries are much older than others, the younger ones will have to withdraw money (and pay tax on it) more quickly than they may wish to.

6. Naming Your Estate

You can name your own estate as the beneficiary of a retirement plan—but doing so ensures that the money in the account will have to go through probate before being distributed. And if you die before age 70½, all the money will have to be withdrawn in five years. If you die after age 70½, whoever inherits the account will have to continue making withdrawals as fast as you would have. So the smart course is simple: don't do it.

7. Naming a Trust

If you've set up a living trust to avoid probate (see Chapter 7), good for you—but your trust should probably not have anything to do with your retirement accounts.

First of all, you don't need a living trust to avoid probate for the money in a retirement account. If you name a beneficiary (as long as you don't name your estate), the money won't go through probate.

If you do name a revocable living trust as the beneficiary of your retirement account, required minimum distributions after your death will be based on the life expectancy of the trust beneficiary (if the beneficiary is a person, not an institution).

8. Naming a Charity or Other Organization

You can name a charity or institution as the beneficiary of your retirement account. While you're alive, minimum required distributions are based on the IRS Uniform table, which assumes that you have a beneficiary ten years younger than you are.

After your death, the charity must take out the money within five years (if you died before you reach 70½) or take distributions based on your life expectancy (if you die after age 70½). Minimum distributions usually aren't a problem for charities, which are happy to cash out the accounts they inherit. But if you name a person and a charity as co-beneficiaries, after your death the IRS treats the situation as if you had not named a beneficiary at all, meaning distributions will be accelerated for the individual beneficiary as well as the charity.

9. Choosing Alternate Beneficiaries

When you name your primary beneficiary, you'll probably be able to name an alternate—someone to inherit the money if your first choice doesn't survive you. Most people who are married with children name their spouse as the primary beneficiary, and the children as the alternates.

It's easy, however, for a beneficiary to "disclaim" his or her inherit-ance—that is, to turn it down in favor of the alternate beneficiary. Why would someone turn down money? An older spouse, for example, simply might not need it. By letting it go to the children instead, with-drawals could be spread out over a longer period.

B. Required Distributions From Retirement Accounts

If you save and invest wisely, you can leave a substantial amount in an individual retirement account—but for most accounts, there are limits. The IRS wants to keep these accounts restricted to their original purpose of providing a decent income during your retirement. You (or your beneficiaries) will be in for severe financial penalties if you violate the rules.

Roth IRAs. There are no required distributions from Roth IRAs. As a result, a Roth IRA could contain a much larger amount at your death than a comparable traditional IRA or 401(k)—and pass that larger amount on without probate.

1. When Withdrawals Must Begin

The ideal scenario, in the eyes of the IRS, would be to have you exhaust the money in your retirement account at precisely the moment you breathe your last. That's why the IRS makes you start withdrawing money in your 70s, and why the amount of these required minimum distributions is tied to your statistical life expectancy.

Traditional IRAs. Distributions become mandatory the year you turn age 70½. (The rules already sound confusing, don't they? It's not too bad—take a deep breath and read on.) The IRS bases everything on calendar years. You must make one whole year's withdrawal for the calendar year in which you turn 70½. This first year, however, you get a bit of extra time before you actually have to take out the money: you have until April 1 of the following year to make the withdrawal. After that, the deadline is always December 31.

Example: *Robert turns 70½ on November 30, 2006. He must make a full year's required minimum distribution for 2006, but he has until April 1, 2007, to do it. He must take 2007's required minimum distribution by December 31, 2007.*

401(k) Accounts. You don't have to withdraw money from your 401(k) account until you turn 70½ or you actually retire, whichever is later. (There's one exception: If you're self-employed, you must begin withdrawals at 70½.) If you retire after you are 70½, then April 1 of the following year is the date by which you must make your first required distribution.

2. Calculating the Minimum Distribution Amount

The minimum amount you must withdraw is based on your life expectancy and that of a beneficiary. The IRS provides a table on which you can look up this "joint life expectancy"; then you simply divide the amount in your account by this number and take out the result.

Example: *Valerie is 75; the IRS Uniform Distribution Period Table gives her a figure of 21.8 years. The balance in her IRA at the end of the previous calendar year was $50,000, so this year she must withdraw $2,294.*

Whether or not you actually name a beneficiary, the IRS table assumes that your beneficiary is ten years younger than you are. You don't need to consider the beneficiary's actual age unless the beneficiary is your spouse and is in fact more than ten years younger than you. In that case, you can reduce the amount you must withdraw by using a different IRS table that factors in your spouse's actual age.

Example 1: *Jason turns 70½ on February 23. That means by April 1 of the next calendar year, he must have made a year's worth of withdrawals from his IRA account. His wife Molly, the beneficiary of the IRA, is four years younger than he is.*

To calculate the minimum amount he must withdraw, Jason will have to look up his age in the IRS Uniform Distribution Table. The table assumes that Molly is ten years younger than Jason, which works to their benefit—the minimum amounts Jason must withdraw each year will be smaller than if Molly's actual life expectancy were used.

Example 2: *Mark names his wife Rita, who is 12 years his junior, as his IRA beneficiary. To calculate his required minimum distribution, he uses the IRS table that calculates his and Rita's joint life expectancy based on their actual ages.*

3. Why You Don't Want to Miss a Required Distribution

If you don't make the legally required withdrawal, you will forfeit half of the amount you should have withdrawn but didn't. That's right: There's a full 50% tax on the money you shouldn't have left in the account.

Example: *When Mae is required to begin taking money from her IRA, she dutifully makes a withdrawal—but mistakenly takes out $1,000 less than she should. The next year, when she files her income tax return, she must pay a $500 extra tax (and file an extra form) on the $1,000 she should have withdrawn.*

RETIREMENT ACCOUNT WITHDRAWAL RULES: A SUMMARY

YOUR AGE	WITHDRAWAL RULES
Younger than 59½ "Premature" withdrawals	**Traditional IRAs:** Withdrawals are subject to a 10% penalty, unless you become disabled and cannot work, you die, you use the money to buy your first house, or you set up a plan to make regular, equal withdrawals over your life. You cannot borrow from an IRA. **Roth IRAs:** Withdrawals of contributions are always tax-free. Qualified withdrawals of earnings are penalty- and tax-free if you've had the account for at least five years and you are disabled or are using the money to buy your first house (up to $10,000). **401(k) plans:** You can borrow from your 401(k), but cannot withdraw money from it except for an IRS-recognized hardship, such as to pay medical bills, prevent eviction or foreclosure, pay college tuition or make a down payment on your primary residence. And you still must pay the 10% penalty on early withdrawals. There is one important exception: If you're 55 or older and actually retired, you may make penalty-free withdrawals.
59½ to 70½ "Ordinary" withdrawals	Withdrawals are optional. **Traditional IRAs:** The amount is included in your gross income for income tax purposes. **Roth IRAs:** Withdrawals of contributions and of qualified earnings are not taxed.

RETIREMENT ACCOUNT WITHDRAWAL RULES: A SUMMARY (CONT.)

70½ or older "Required" distributions	**Traditional IRAs and 401(k)s:** Withdrawals are required. The minimum amount is determined by your age. **Roth IRAs:** Withdrawals are optional.

More information. *IRAs, 401(k)s & Other Retirement Plans: Taking Your Money Out,* by Twila Slesnick and John C. Suttle (Nolo). A thorough discussion of the rules that govern withdrawals from the most common kinds of retirement plans.

Decisions When Retiring, by Holmes Crouch (Allyear Tax Guides). Practical, idiosyncratic advice about retirement as well as nuts-and-bolts tax information.

The website www.rothira.com contains news, articles, calculators, links, and much more, all dealing with various aspects of the Roth IRA.

■

CHAPTER 3

Name a Beneficiary for Stocks and Bonds

Several factors have combined to produce a tremendous flood of money into the stock market in the last few decades. Many working people, suddenly in charge of their own retirement investments, began to store up money in IRAs and 401(k) plans, and invested the funds in the market. Investing in stocks or bonds became simpler and less risky with the advent of widely advertised mutual funds, with their diversified holdings. And discount brokers made buying and selling individual stocks less costly.

As a result, many ordinary Americans now have sizable amounts tied up in corporate and government securities instead of plain old bank accounts, savings bonds, or certificates of deposit. To their credit, state lawmakers have responded to this important shift with what passes for lightning speed in the legislative world. In fewer than ten years, almost every state has authorized a simple way for people to leave securities to their loved ones without probate.

A. Transfer-on-Death Registration

Every state except Louisiana and Texas has adopted a law that lets you name someone to inherit your stocks, bonds, or brokerage accounts without probate. It works very much like a payable-on-death bank account (explained in Chapter 1). When you register your ownership, either with the stockbroker or the company itself, you make a request to take ownership in what's called "beneficiary form." When the papers that show your ownership are issued, they will also show the name of your beneficiary.

After you have registered ownership this way, the beneficiary has no rights to the stock as long as you are alive. You are free to sell it, give it away, name a different beneficiary, or close the account. But on your death, the beneficiary can claim the securities without probate, simply by providing proof of death and some identification to the broker or transfer agent. (A transfer agent is a business that is authorized by a corporation to transfer ownership of its stock from one person to another.)

The law that allows transfer-on-death registration is called the Uniform Transfer-on-Death Securities Registration Act.

BENEFICIARY REGISTRATION AT A GLANCE

Pros	Cons
• Easy to create.	• Your broker might not allow you to name an alternate beneficiary.
• Designating a beneficiary costs nothing (though some brokers may charge a fee to change beneficiaries)	
• It's easy for the beneficiary to claim the securities after the original owner dies.	

---

1. Who Can Use the Law

If you live in any state but Louisiana or Texas, you can register any stocks or mutual fund shares in beneficiary form. Even if you live in a different state, however, you may be able to register your stocks in a transfer-on-death form. That's because the way the law is written, if either the stock owner or the stock issuer has any connection to a state that has passed the law, transfer-on-death registration is available.

You can register ownership of a stock or a mutual fund account in beneficiary form if *any* of the following is true:

- You live in a state that has adopted the law.
- The stockbroker's principal office is located in a state that has adopted the law.
- The issuer of the stock or the stockbroker ("registering entity") is incorporated in a state that has adopted the law.
- The transfer agent's office is located in a state that has adopted the law.
- The office making the registration is in a state that has adopted the law.

Example 1: *Sophia is a resident of Florida, which has adopted the Transfer-on-Death Security Registration Act. She can register any stock or brokerage account she owns in beneficiary form, regardless of where the company that issues or registers the stock is located.*

Example 2: *Ben lives in Texas, which has not passed the Act. But he maintains a brokerage account with Cascade Mutual Fund, which has its main office in the state of Washington, which has adopted the Act. He can name a transfer-on-death beneficiary and avoid probate of the account.*

Example 3: *Ben also owns some stock of the Olde Cudahy Cheese Works, Inc., a company incorporated in Wisconsin. Because Wisconsin has adopted the Act, Ben can register ownership of his shares in beneficiary form.*

Your broker may not cooperate. Although a good many stockbrokers, corporations, and transfer agents offer transfer-on-death registration, the law does not require them to; it merely gives them the option of doing so. If your state passed the uniform law recently, you may even have to educate your broker about it—or, if that fails, move your account.

2. How It Works

It's a simple process to register ownership of your stocks in beneficiary (also called transfer-on-death, or T.O.D.) form. The exact procedure, however, depends on whether you hold your stocks in a brokerage account or you actually have stock certificates sent to you.

If you have a brokerage account (or more than one, as many people do), you should contact the broker for instructions. Most likely, the broker will send you a form on which you'll name one or more beneficiaries to inherit the stocks in your account at your death. From then on, the account will be listed in your name, with the beneficiary's name after it, like this:

"Evelyn M. Meyers, T.O.D. Charles Meyers."

If you have the actual stock certificates or bonds in your possession—most people don't—you must get new certificates issued, showing that you now own the stock in beneficiary form. Ask your broker for help. If the broker is unable or unwilling to help, write to the transfer agent for the stock. You can get the address from your broker or the investor relations office of the corporation. The transfer agent will explain what to do. You'll probably have to send in the certificates and a form called a stock or bond power, which you must fill out and sign (some stock certificates have the power printed on the back) and a letter explaining what you want to do.

GIFT AND ESTATE TAX CONCERNS

You keep complete control over the securities for which you name a transfer-on-death beneficiary, so you're not, in legal terms, making a gift when you register stocks in beneficiary form. That means you don't have to worry about federal gift tax.

Naming a beneficiary has no effect on federal estate taxes, either. At your death, the value of the stocks is included in your estate for federal estate tax purposes, just as it would have been had you not named a transfer-on-death beneficiary.

3. Joint Accounts

If you own stock or mutual fund shares together with another person—your wife or husband, for example—you can still name a transfer-on-death beneficiary. But there's an important restriction: You and the co-owner must have "rights of survivorship" in the account. That means that when the first owner dies, the survivor automatically takes full ownership. That's how most joint accounts are set up. The transfer-on-death beneficiary inherits the stock only after both original owners have died.

Incidentally, this also takes care of a common concern of many couples: what will happen if they die simultaneously.

Example: *Helen and Chase own a mutual fund account together. On the account documents, their names are listed this way: "Helen Whittaker, Chase Whittaker JT TEN WROS." That means that they own the account as joint tenants with the right of survivorship—the legal way of saying that they share ownership 50-50, and when Helen or Chase dies, the survivor will automatically own the entire account.*

When Helen and Chase decide to add their grown children, Amanda and Jeffrey, as transfer-on-death beneficiaries, the ownership documents are changed to include this odd-looking string of words: "Helen Whittaker, Chase Whittaker JT TEN WROS, TOD Amanda S. Whittaker and Jeffrey R. Whittaker." The T.O.D. stands for "transfer on death."

After one joint owner dies, the other is free to change the beneficiary designation. So naming a T.O.D. beneficiary while both joint owners are alive doesn't guarantee that that beneficiary will ultimately inherit the securities.

Example: *Jane and Henry name Henry's son from a previous marriage as the T.O.D. beneficiary of a jointly held stock account. After Henry dies, Jane is the sole owner, and decides to change the beneficiary to someone else. Henry's son won't inherit any of the stocks.*

You can lock in a beneficiary. If you're concerned that after your death, the surviving co-owner of a joint account might change the beneficiary in a way you wouldn't approve of, create a separate account in your name only, and name the beneficiary. (But if you're married, you should still get your spouse's consent; see Section 4, next.)

4. Your Spouse's Rights

You may not have complete freedom to dispose of your securities—even if they're registered in your name—as you wish. Your spouse may have rights, too. The extent of those rights depends on your state's law.

COMMUNITY PROPERTY STATES		NON-COMMUNITY PROPERTY STATES
Alaska*	Nevada	All other states
Arizona	New Mexico	
California	Texas	
Idaho	Washington	
Louisiana	Wisconsin	

*Only if spouses sign a community property agreement.

a. Spouses' Rights in Community Property States

If you live in a community property state, your spouse may well own half of whatever securities you own, even if you hold them in your name only. If you bought securities with money you earned while married, they are "community property," and your spouse legally owns a half-share unless you and your spouse signed a valid agreement to keep all your property separate.

 Domestic partners. California is the only state that allows registered domestic partners to own community property.

If you have a securities account registered in your name only, and you want to name someone other than your spouse as the T.O.D. beneficiary for it, it's a good idea to get your spouse's written consent. Otherwise, if your spouse objects, he or she could assert a claim to half of the money in the account at your death, leaving the beneficiary you named with only half.

b. Spouses' Rights in Non-Community Property States

If you leave stocks to someone other than your spouse, make sure your spouse doesn't object to your overall estate plan.

In non-community property states, surviving spouses who are unhappy with what the deceased spouse left them can claim a certain percentage of the deceased spouse's property. This is called the spouse's "statutory share," and in many states it amounts to about a third of what the spouse owned. It's rare, however, for a spouse to go to court over this, because most spouses inherit more than their statutory share.

The funds in a T.O.D. account may be subject to a spouse's claim— or they may not, depending on state law. Some states consider such accounts outside the surviving spouse's reach.

5. Naming Children as Beneficiaries

You can name a minor—that is, a child younger than 18 years old—as a transfer-on-death beneficiary, but doing so raises some legal issues you should deal with. Every state's law forbids children younger than 18 from controlling substantial amounts of property themselves, without an adult's supervision. The dollar limit varies from state to state, but it's fair to say that anything worth more than a few thousand dollars necessitates an adult manager for the money.

Fortunately, it's not difficult to take care of this potential complication. You can choose someone, now, to manage the money if the beneficiary you've chosen inherits the money while still a minor. In most states, you can appoint this person on the registration document by naming him or her as a "custodian" of the property.

Example: *Tess wants to leave stock to her ten-year-old nephew, Sam, but wants his mother to manage it in case Sam inherits it while he is still a child. On the ownership registration document, she names the T.O.D. beneficiary as "Amelia Tompkins, as custodian for Samuel Tompkins under the Indiana Uniform Transfers to Minors Act."*

For more detailed information about custodianship under the Uniform Transfers to Minors Act, see Chapter 1, Section C.

6. Naming More Than One T.O.D. Beneficiary

If you want to name more than one beneficiary, just name all the beneficiaries on the form. Each will inherit an equal share of the stocks unless you specify otherwise. You can, however, leave the beneficiaries unequal shares if the stockbroker or transfer agent's policy allows it. (If you do, double-check your percentages and make sure they add up to 100%, or the fractions to 1. It's easier than you might think to make a mistake.)

Example: *Martha lists her four children as the T.O.D. beneficiaries of her mutual fund shares. She decides to leave one of her children, who has a disabled child and could use more financial help, a larger share than the rest. She registers ownership of the mutual fund shares this way: "Martha Levenson, TOD Frank Levenson 20%, Elizabeth Levenson 20%, Emily Levenson-Thompson 20%, David Levenson 40%."*

7. If a Beneficiary Dies Before You Do

You can name an alternate beneficiary, if your broker's policies allow it, when you register securities in transfer-on-death form. If you do, and the primary T.O.D. beneficiary dies before you do, the alternate will inherit.

Example: *Francis names his wife as the T.O.D. beneficiary of his mutual fund account and his daughter Marie as contingent (alternate) beneficiary. His wife dies, and Francis doesn't get around to changing the paperwork to name a new beneficiary. When Francis dies, the account goes to Marie.*

If you don't name an alternate, the stock would probably pass under your will's "residuary clause," which names a beneficiary to inherit everything that's not specifically mentioned in the will. Your "residuary beneficiary" would inherit the securities.

If you name more than one beneficiary, and one or more of them dies before you do, the securities will go to the survivor(s) at your death.

Example: *Cheryl's children, Zachary and Grace, are the T.O.D. beneficiaries of her brokerage account. Zachary dies before Cheryl does, leaving three children of his own. If Cheryl wants these grandchildren to inherit their father's share, she must change her account registration papers to include them as T.O.D. beneficiaries. Otherwise, at her death, the account will belong solely to Grace.*

8. If You Change Your Mind

You are always free to change the T.O.D. beneficiary of your securities. The beneficiary's consent—or knowledge—is not required. To make a change, contact the broker or transfer agent. You must redo the ownership document itself for the change to take effect.

9. When Not to Use T.O.D. Registration

As useful as it can be, T.O.D. registration is not always a good idea. In general, stay away from it if you want to name multiple beneficiaries and the securities aren't easily divisible. Trying to divide a single bond, for example, among three children can get very worky.

10. Claiming the Securities

After your death, all the beneficiary needs to do to claim the stocks is show the transfer agent or broker a certified copy of the death certificate and proof of his or her identity. If the account was a joint account to begin with and wasn't ever changed to the name of the survivor, the beneficiary will need the death certificates of all the original owners. The broker's or transfer agent's records themselves will show that the beneficiary is entitled to the securities.

Once the broker has the necessary documents, the securities or the account can be reregistered in the new owner's name. No probate court approval is required. Legally, the securities automatically belong to the beneficiaries when the original owner dies.

B. Registration of Government Bonds and Notes

You can also name someone to inherit certain kinds of government securities, including Treasury bills and notes and savings bonds.

To do this, register ownership of the securities in "beneficiary" form. You simply register ownership in your name, followed by the words "payable on death to" and the name of your beneficiary. The beneficiary must be a person, not an organization. (31 C.F.R. Parts 315.6 and 353.6.) If the beneficiary is a minor, you must specify that—for example, by writing "payable on death to Jasmine Martin, a minor." After your death, ownership will be transferred to the person you named.

As with corporate securities, you'll have complete control over these assets. You don't need the beneficiary's consent to sell or give away the securities, and you can name a different beneficiary at any time by filling out new ownership documents.

One significant limitation on adding a payable-on-death beneficiary is that there may be only one primary owner and one beneficiary. You can't name a payable-on-death beneficiary if the securities are co-owned by two or more people—you and your spouse, for example. In that situation, the best you can do is to create a right of survivorship, so that the surviving co-owner inherits the securities when the first co-owner dies. Then, the survivor could add a beneficiary designation.

Example: *Marilyn and Richard buy Treasury bonds and notes, and hold title to their account as "Marilyn Vanderburg and Richard Vanderburg, with right of survivorship." Many years later, after Marilyn's death, Richard changes the title to add their adult daughter as the beneficiary. Now, the title is held as "Richard Vanderburg, payable on death to Melissa Vanderburg."*

Also, you cannot name an alternate beneficiary to inherit the bonds if your first choice does not survive you.

If naming an alternate is important to you, think twice about using the beneficiary form of registration. If you want to name a specific alternate to inherit your government securities without probate, you'll need to use another probate-avoidance method, such as a living trust. (See Chapter 7.) Before you get too concerned, though, weigh several factors, including:

- Your age, and that of your beneficiary. If your primary beneficiary died, do you think you would be able to handle the paperwork to name another beneficiary?
- The value of the securities. If the securities went through probate, would that impose a large expense on whoever inherits them?
- The person you've chosen as your residuary beneficiary of your will. If you're happy with that person as a backup beneficiary, you don't have a problem.

BUYING GOVERNMENT SECURITIES

If you want to buy government securities directly, not through a broker, contact a Federal Reserve Bank servicing office. Every large city has one, as do a fair number of medium-sized cities.

Ask for a Treasury Direct Tender package. It should contain a booklet called Buying Treasury Securities and copies of the forms you need.

For online information about savings bonds, T-bills, notes, and bonds, check out www.publicdebt.treas.gov.

CHAPTER 4

Name a Beneficiary for Your Vehicles

Probate is spectacularly unsuited to cars and other vehicles. Given their maintenance requirements and rapid depreciation, it makes absolutely no sense to have them sitting around for months or years while probate grinds on, before they can be transferred to their new owners.

This chapter discusses a few ways to make sure that a car will get to the person you want to inherit it quickly and easily, without formal probate proceedings.

A. Transfer-on-Death Registration

 Skip ahead. If you don't own a car registered in California, Connecticut, Kansas, Missouri, or Ohio, you can skip to Section B.

So far, only a few states offer car owners the sensible option of naming a beneficiary, right on the registration form, to inherit the vehicle. The practice should spread; it's a simple, effective way for folks to pass on their cars, trucks, and small boats. Meanwhile, beause so many vehicles are registered in car-choked California, this option is actually available to a sizable number of the country's drivers.

BENEFICIARY REGISTRATION AT A GLANCE

Pros	Cons
• Easy and free to set up.	• Can't name an alternate
• You can change your mind at any time.	beneficiary.
	• Available only in California, Connecticut, Kansas, Missouri, and Ohio.

1. How It Works

The process is simplicity itself. All you do is apply for a certificate of car ownership in "beneficiary form." The fee is the same as for a standard certificate. The new certificate lists the name of the beneficiary (or more than one), who will automatically own the vehicle after your death.

The beneficiary you name has no rights as long as you are alive. You are free to sell or give away the car, or name someone else as the beneficiary.

In Kansas and Missouri, if you own the vehicle with someone else—say, your spouse—you can still designate a beneficiary. The beneficiary will inherit the vehicle only after both you and the other owner have died. (Kan. Stat. Ann. § 59-3508; Mo. Rev. Stat. § 301.681.) In California, Connecticut, and Ohio, however, transfer-on-death registration is limited to one owner. (Cal. Veh. Code § 4150.7; Conn. Gen. Stat. Ann. § 14-16; Ohio Rev. Code Ann. § 2131.13.) So you may want to own the vehicle in joint tenancy with the other owner now, which will avoid probate at the first owner's death. Then the sole surviving owner can designate a beneficiary to inherit the car without probate.

AVOIDING PROBATE FOR SMALL BOATS

In California and Ohio, the beneficiary form of registration is also available for small boats. (Cal. Veh. Code § 9852.7; Ohio Rev. Code Ann. § 2131.13.) The rules are generally the same as those that apply to other motor vehicles.

⚠ **In California, get your spouse's (or registered domestic partner's) consent before naming someone else as beneficiary.** In California, a community property state, your spouse may own a half-interest in a vehicle even if it's registered in your name. If you bought it with money you earned while married (or in a registered domestic partnership), it's "community property," and you and your mate own it 50-50 unless you have both signed a written agreement to the contrary.

If the vehicle is community property, and you want to name someone other than your spouse as the beneficiary, get your spouse's written consent—and store it with your title slips and other important documents where they can be found after your death.

2. If You Change Your Mind

You are free to revoke a beneficiary designation at any time, but there are restrictions on how you can do it. Only two ways, in fact, are allowed. You can either:

- sell the vehicle, or
- apply for a new certificate of ownership, one that does not name a beneficiary at all or names a different one.

You cannot revoke the beneficiary provision by leaving the car to someone else in your will or living trust. If you try, your efforts won't have any effect.

Example: *Claudia, a Californian, registers her car in beneficiary form, naming her niece Arlene to inherit it. Later, after the two have a falling-out, Claudia writes a will leaving the car to her friend Hal. At Claudia's death, the car will belong to Arlene, despite the will provision to the contrary.*

3. Transferring Title After Death

When the owner dies, the vehicle belongs to the beneficiary listed on the certificate of ownership. To reregister the vehicle in his or her own name, the new owner must submit to the state motor vehicles agency several documents:

- an application for the new certificate
- the old certificate of ownership, if available, and
- a death certificate to prove that the former owner has died.

Once the new owner turns in these documents and pays the required fee, the state agency will issue a new certificate of ownership.

The beneficiary inherits any outstanding debts on the vehicle, as well as the vehicle. So if your car isn't paid off at your death, the beneficiary will inherit your obligation to repay the loan.

B. Joint Ownership With the Right of Survivorship

If you're part of a couple—married or not—it's often smart to hold title to your cars together, as "joint tenants with the right of survivorship." That way, when one owner dies, the other will own the vehicle, without probate.

In some states (Oregon, for example), you don't have to add any magic words to the title document: If you own a car jointly with someone else, and one of you dies, the survivor automatically owns the car. In Kentucky, that's true only if the co-owners are husband and wife.

In most states, however, you must take some care to set up the ownership in a way that will let the survivor inherit the car without probate. Usually, the car registration document must spell out that you own the car "in joint tenancy with right of survivorship." When you go to register your car, your state's motor vehicles agency should be able to tell you what words to use to achieve the result you want. Texas includes on its certificates of title a "Rights of Survivorship Agreement Form," for husbands and wives to sign.

After one owner dies, the surviving owner automatically owns the vehicle. But the new sole owner must still reregister title in his or her name alone. This process is sometimes called clearing title. Usually, it's quite easy; all that the state motor vehicles department requires is a written statement from the new owner (the state may provide a fill-in-the-blanks form) and proof of death (a death certificate). Some states issue a new certificate of ownership for free in these circumstances.

⚠️ **Be cautious about adding a co-owner just to avoid probate.** Many single, older people are tempted to make someone—a grown son or daughter, perhaps—the joint owner of a car, solely for the purpose of avoiding probate. But in many instances, that's not a good idea. Keep in mind that you're giving away a half-interest in the car, which can have several undesirable consequences:

- If you change your mind, you can't get the half-interest back unless the other co-owner agrees; a gift is permanent.

- If the co-owner is on the losing end of a lawsuit or files for bankruptcy, a creditor could seize his or her interest in the car.

- If the half-interest is worth more than the amount of the annual federal gift tax exclusion (currently $12,000), you are required to file a federal gift tax return. No gift tax will actually be due, however, unless at your death you have given away or left such a large amount of property that you have exceeded the gift and estate tax threshold, as explained in Chapter 9. (And given how quickly new cars plummet in value after they're driven off the dealer's lot, gift tax should be a concern only if you're sharing a spanking new car.)

(Joint tenancy is discussed further in Chapter 6.)

C. Special Transfer Procedures for Vehicles

Even if your state doesn't let you register vehicles in transfer-on-death form, and you don't own it in joint tenancy, the person who inherits your car—through your will, for example—may still be able to take title to it without probate court proceedings.

It depends on where you live. Some states have special nonprobate transfer procedures just for vehicles. All the new owner must do is complete a simple written statement (affidavit) setting out some basic facts, sign it in front of a notary public, and file it with the state agency that registers vehicles. For example, in Hawaii, a vehicle, regardless of value, can be transferred to its new owner by affidavit. (Haw. Rev. Stat. § 560:3-1201.) In Utah, up to four vehicles can be transferred this way if the rest of the deceased person's estate is worth $25,000 or less. (Utah Code Ann. § 75-3-1201.)

But in many states, there's an important restriction: the affidavit procedure is available only if probate isn't necessary for any of your other assets. If a regular probate proceeding is going on, the car must go through that process. If you want to know the specifics of your state's paperwork, contact a local office of the state motor vehicles agency.

WHERE SPOUSES HAVE IT EASY

In Maine, if a married person dies owning any vehicles registered in that state, they automatically pass to the surviving spouse unless a will provides otherwise (or someone who has a legal claim on the car, such as a loan company, refuses to consent). Registration and title are transferred to the surviving spouse with no fee or tax. (Me. Rev. Stat. Ann. tit. 29-A, § 663.)

Similarly, in New York, ownership of a single car worth no more than $15,000 automatically goes to the surviving spouse. In Ohio, a surviving spouse automatically gets up to two cars, without probate, unless the deceased spouse left them to someone else by will or T.O.D. registration. (Ohio Rev. Code § 2106.18.)

Michigan also has a special rule for spouses. A surviving spouse (or heir if there is no spouse and no will) can claim a vehicle without probate if:

- the deceased spouse left vehicles with a total value of less than $60,000, and
- no other assets require regular probate.

The spouse applies to the Secretary of State for a new title. (Mich. Comp. Laws Ann. § 257.236.)

These are just examples. You may want to check your own state's laws for procedures your family could take advantage of.

Example: *Graham, an Oregon resident, dies owning a house, car, several mutual fund accounts, a bank account, individual retirement account (IRA), and some household furnishings and personal belongings.*

Before his death, Graham named pay-on-death beneficiaries for his mutual fund accounts and IRA. He and his wife held their house in tenancy by the entirety and a bank account in joint tenancy with right of survivorship. In his will, he left his personal belongings to his wife and his car to his son.

Whether or not the car qualifies for the affidavit procedure depends on whether probate is required for the rest of Graham's estate. Here's how it breaks down:

Asset	Probate necessary?
House	*No, because owned in tenancy by the entirety with his wife.*
Personal belongings	*No, because value isn't high enough to necessitate probate under Oregon law.*
IRA, mutual funds	*No, because Graham named pay-on-death beneficiary.*
Bank account	*No, because held in joint tenancy with right of survivorship with his wife.*
Car	*No, because probate is not necessary for any other property. Graham's son can file a simple form with the state Motor Vehicles Division and immediately take title to the car.*

If the simplified procedure is available, your state's motor vehicles department may provide a form for the inheritors to fill out and file. The Oregon affidavit form is shown below.

If there isn't an official form, the person who inherits a vehicle will have to write up an affidavit (a sworn statement, signed in front of a notary public), including whatever information the state law then requires. For example, the affidavit might need to state that no probate proceedings are underway or planned, and list all the known heirs of the deceased person.

Finding out exactly what's required in the affidavit may require looking up the state statute that sets out the specific requirements. You can find your state's statutes at any public law library (available in most courthouses) or online. To look up a statute on the Web, start at the part of the Nolo website, www.nolo.com/statute, that links to all states' statutes. If you're lucky, your state's website will offer you a table of contents. Start here and look for the sections about vehicles or probate. If that's not available, you can probably search for a particular word.

SAMPLE OREGON FORM

DEPARTMENT OF TRANSPORTATION
DRIVER AND MOTOR VEHICLE SERVICES
1905 LANA AVE NE, SALEM OR 97314

INHERITANCE AFFIDAVIT

If a deceased owner's estate is not probated, their interest in a vehicle may be assigned through the use of this affidavit signed by all the heirs of the owner(s) stating the name of the person to whom the ownership interest has been assigned. (ORS 803.094)

This form must be submitted to DMV with the title (if available), application for title, and title transfer fee.

- **DMV must receive an affidavit completed and signed by all heirs.** Heirs are determined according to ORS Chapter 112. DMV cannot determine the heirs for you. You may wish to seek legal counsel to determine who the heirs are.

- If there is more than one heir, the heirs may either complete and sign the same affidavit or complete and sign separate affidavits. Each affidavit must indicate to whom ownership of the vehicle is assigned.

- If there are no other heirs, leave the space provided below, for listing heirs, blank.

- If the heir is a minor or is incapacitated, the parent or guardian must sign for the heir. (Example: Jane Q. Public, age 10, by *John Q. Public*, parent.) If the guardian signs, a copy of the court papers showing guardianship must be submitted with the affidavit.

- The affidavit must be signed before a notary. (The notary does not have to be from the State of Oregon.)

I/We, _____

declare that _____

died on the _____ day of _____ , 20 _____ ; and that the estate has not

and will not be probated.

At the time of death, the deceased was the owner of the following described vehicle:

PLATE NUMBER	YEAR	MAKE	VEHICLE IDENTIFICATION NUMBER

List all heirs. (Any heirs not signing this affidavit must complete a separate affidavit.) **I certify if there are no names listed below, there are no other heirs.**

I/we release any and all claim to the following party:

NAME OF PERSON TO WHOM OWNERSHIP OF THE VEHICLE HAS BEEN ASSIGNED.	ADDRESS	
CITY	STATE	ZIP CODE

ALL HEIRS MUST SIGN BELOW

SIGNATURE OF HEIR	SIGNATURE OF HEIR
X	X
SIGNATURE OF HEIR	SIGNATURE OF HEIR
X	X

NOTARY

State of _____ County of _____

Subscribed and sworn before me this _____ day of _____, 20 ____

by _____.

X _____
   SIGNATURE OF NOTARY PUBLIC

Some states charge the regular fee to issue a new certificate of ownership; others do it for free.

LAWYERS GET THEIR SHARE IN ILLINOIS

Even if you avoid probate in Illinois, the law makes it impossible to avoid lawyers. When it comes to transferring a vehicle, the new owner's sworn statement isn't good enough; an affidavit signed by an attorney at law and "on the letterhead stationery of the attorney" must be submitted to the Secretary of State, who will then transfer title to the vehicle to the new owner. (625 Ill. Comp. Stat. § 5/3-114.)

Don't overlook simple procedures for small estates. Even if your state does not have a special transfer procedure just for vehicles, your inheritors may still be able to transfer a vehicle—and everything else you leave—without probate if the value of your estate is small enough. (See Chapter 8.)

CHAPTER 5

Name a Beneficiary for Your Real Estate

For most homeowners, keeping a house out of probate is their biggest probate-avoidance wish—and challenge. A living trust works well, but not everyone wants to go to the expense and trouble of creating one. And joint tenancy isn't always the best option, either. Here's good news: Several states now offer an easy and effective alternative for real estate within their borders, and other states are considering adopting it.

This alternative is called a transfer-on-death deed or beneficiary deed. It's like a regular deed used to transfer real estate, with a crucial difference: It doesn't take effect until your death.

TRANSFER-ON-DEATH DEEDS AT A GLANCE

Pros	Cons
• Easy to create, usually	• You may need a lawyer to help
• You can change your mind	you prepare a deed valid
at any time	in your state
• After your death, easy for	
beneficiary to transfer title	

A. Can You Use a T.O.D. Deed?

If you own real estate in any of the states listed below, you can use a T.O.D. deed to leave that real estate to someone. No other states allow these kinds of deeds yet.

If you try to leave property in another state by deed at your death, it won't work. For example, if you sign a deed transferring your house to your children and stick it in your desk drawer, knowing that they will find it there after your death, the deed won't have any effect. A deed is not a valid substitute for a will (which must be signed in front of witnesses) unless state law specifically allows it.

STATES THAT AUTHORIZE TRANSFER-ON-DEATH DEEDS

Arizona	Ariz. Rev. Stat. Ann. § 33-405
Arkansas	Ark. Code Ann. § 18-12-608
Colorado	Colo. Rev. Stat. § 15-15-402
Kansas	Kan. Stat. § 59-3501
Missouri	Mo. Rev. Stat. § 461.025
Nevada	Nev. Rev. Stat. § 111.109
New Mexico	N.M. Stat. Ann. § 45-6-401
Ohio	Ohio Rev. Code § 5302.22

B. How It Works: An Overview

Using a transfer-on-death deed is a lot like using a payable-on-death designation for a bank account. You name one or more beneficiaries now, who then inherit the property at your death without the need for probate court proceedings.

To name a beneficiary, you use a special kind of deed, one that's tailored to the law of your state. The deed looks pretty much like any other real estate deed; it shows who owns the property, who it's being transferred to, and describes the property exactly. But a T.O.D. deed contains an additional statement, making it clear that the deed does not take effect until the current owner's death. A sample deed, from Colorado, is shown below.

The beneficiary you name to inherit the property doesn't have any legal right to it until your death—or, if you own the property with your spouse or someone else, until the last surviving owner dies. The beneficiary doesn't have to sign, acknowledge, or even be told about the deed.

In the deed, you can also name an alternate beneficiary who will inherit the real estate if your first choice isn't alive at your death. If you don't name an alternate, and your first choice doesn't survive you, state law determines who will inherit the property.

After you've signed the deed, you must record it with the local county land records office before your death. Otherwise, it won't be valid.

You keep complete ownership of and control over the property while you're alive. You pay the taxes on it, and it's not protected from your creditors. You can sell it, give it away, or mortgage it. Because the T.O.D. deed does not make a gift of the property, there's no need to concern yourself with gift tax.

Later, if you change your mind about who you want to inherit the property, you are not locked in. You can revoke the T.O.D. deed or simply record another T.O.D. deed, leaving the property to someone else.

At your death, ownership passes immediately—and automatically—to the beneficiary you named in the deed. Any mortgage or debt attached to the land goes along with it. The new owner will, at most, have to record a sworn statement (affidavit) and a copy of the death certificate. The process is definitely much simpler and quicker than probate.

Watch out for your state's special rules. Every state has its own rules about T.O.D. deeds, and some of these may be important. For example, in Colorado, recording a T.O.D. deed disqualifies you from receiving Medicaid (so if you ever need coverage, you'll need to revoke the deed, or have authorized someone to do it on your behalf). Before you set off to prepare your deed, read your state's statute yourself (see below for a tip on how to find it) or consult a knowledgeable lawyer—or do both.

C. How to Prepare, Sign, and Record the Deed

Here's where you need to be careful. If your deed doesn't contain the right language, isn't formatted in the correct way, or isn't notarized properly, it won't work. A deed is a simple, one-page document, and it isn't hard to get it right—you just have to pay close attention to your state's requirements.

1. Get a Deed Form or Prepare Your Own

You can buy a fill-in-the-blanks deed form or type up your own docu-ment. State-specific T.O.D. deed forms are available online and in some office supply stores. Be sure any form you use meets the requirements of your state's T.O.D. deed statute. Many of these statutes specify just what language the deed must contain.

Finding your state's statute. You can find the most recent version of your state's statute online, using the citation given above. Start at www.nolo.com/statute.

You must also format the deed so that it will be acceptable for recording in the local land records office. For example, you'll have to leave a certain amount of space at the top of the page for the recording information that the clerk will add to the document. You can find out all the requirements from the recording office ahead of time.

2. Name the Beneficiary

You can name anyone you please to inherit your real estate—a person, more than one person, or an organization such as a favorite charity. Your choice is called the "grantee-beneficiary" in most states. You can also name an alternate beneficiary, commonly called a "successor grantee-beneficiary."

Name each beneficiary specifically; don't use categories such as "my nieces and nephews." If you want to leave your house to your two children, then on the deed you should put, for example, "Robert P. Wyman and Rosamund M. Wyman," not "my children." In some states a deed left to a category of beneficiaries simply isn't valid; in others, it will be confusing at best.

If you name more than one beneficiary, choose how they will take title to the property. For example, you may want to leave it to them "as joint tenants," meaning that when one dies, the surviving co-owners will automatically own the property. But each state has its own options—for example, a few states don't recognize the term "joint tenants." You'll need to find out what your choices are, and their pros and cons. If the beneficiaries want a different arrangement, they can change the way they hold title once they own the property.

3. Describe the Property

Copy the exact description of the property—carefully—from your current deed. Then check it over at least once.

4. Sign the Deed

If you own the property alone, you're probably the only person who needs to sign the deed.

There's one exception: If you live in a community property state, both you and your spouse should sign the deed, just to make it clear that your spouse doesn't object.

If you think your spouse might revoke the deed later, see a lawyer. If you have any reason to think that if you died first, your spouse would claim ownership of the property and revoke the transfer-on-death deed, frustrating your wish to have it go to the T.O.D. beneficiary, see a lawyer before you prepare a T.O.D. deed.

If you own the property with someone else, you should both sign the deed. The T.O.D. deed will not take effect until the last surviving owner dies.

Example: *Jack and Maureen own their house together as joint tenants, which means that when one of them dies, the survivor will automatically own the property. They sign and record a T.O.D. deed, leaving the property to their adult son Ryan at their death. After Jack dies, Maureen owns the property alone. At her death, it goes to Ryan.*

If only one co-owner signs a T.O.D. deed, it will have no effect unless that co-owner is the last surviving owner.

Notarization. You must sign the deed in front of a notary public. That means you need a notarization statement (commonly called an "acknowledgment") at the bottom of the deed, which the notary will fill in and sign.

5. Record the Deed

Your deed is no good until it's recorded (filed) in the local public records. To get that done, take the signed deed to the land records office for the county in which the real estate is located. This office is commonly called the county recorder, land registry, or registrar of deeds. If you aren't sure, call the courthouse and ask where to record deeds.

You'll have to pay a small fee for recording. The clerk will stamp some recording information on the deed, make a copy for the public records, and return the original to you.

SAMPLE TRANSFER-ON-DEATH DEED (COLORADO)

BENEFICIARY DEED

CAUTION: THIS DEED MUST BE RECORDED PRIOR TO THE DEATH OF THE GRANTOR IN ORDER TO BE EFFECTIVE.

Julius M. Benjamin, as grantor, designates Madison R. Benjamin as grantee-beneficiary, whose address is 1234 N. Elm Street, Denver, Colorado, (Note to Assessor and Treasurer: This address is for identification purposes only; all notices and tax statements should continue to be sent to grantor.) or if grantee-beneficiary fails to survive grantor, grantor designates Henry H. Harrison as successor grantee-beneficiary, whose address is 8877 Berry Lane, Denver, Colorado, and grantor transfers, sells, and conveys on grantor's death to the grantee-beneficiary, the following described real property located in the County of Denver, State of Colorado:

W 46FT OF S 70FT & W 45FT OF N 30FT OF PLOT 1 BLK 35 ARMANS… [Remainder of legal description would go here.]

Known and numbered as 1831 W. Maple Ave., Denver, Colorado.

THIS BENEFICIARY DEED IS REVOCABLE. IT DOES NOT TRANSFER ANY OWNERSHIP UNTIL THE DEATH OF THE GRANTOR. IT REVOKES ALL PRIOR BENEFICIARY DEEDS BY THIS GRANTOR FOR THIS REAL PROPERTY EVEN IF THE BENEFICIARY DEED FAILS TO CONVEY ALL OF THE GRANTOR'S INTEREST IN THIS REAL PROPERTY.

WARNING: EXECUTION OF THIS BENEFICIARY DEED MAY DISQUALIFY THE GRANTOR FROM BEING DETERMINED ELIGIBLE FOR, OR FROM RECEIVING MEDICAID UNDER TITLE 26, COLORADO REVISED STATUTES.

WARNING: EXECUTION OF THIS BENEFICIARY DEED MAY NOT AVOID PROBATE.

Executed this _____*November 30, 20xx*_____

_____*Julius M. Benjamin*_____
(Grantor)

[notarization]

D. Three Ways to Cancel the Deed—and One Way Not To

You can always change your mind after you record a T.O.D. deed. The beneficiary has absolutely no rights over the property until after your death.

But first, a caution: Don't use your will to try to revoke a transfer-on-death deed. It won't work.

Example: *Betty records a T.O.D. deed leaving her house to her niece Emily, who has been a great help to her during a serious illness. In her will, she leaves everything else to her son, who lives far away. Years later, when Betty gets around to revising her will, she decides that her son should inherit the house after all. In her will, she states that he is to inherit the house.*

When Betty dies, Emily will automatically own the house, despite what the will says. The will has no effect on the recorded deed.

1. Record a Revocation

The clearest way to make your intention clear is to sign a simple document revoking the T.O.D. deed and record it just like you recorded the original deed. Then the public records show that the deed was revoked. A sample revocation (taken from the Arkansas statute) is shown below.

Generally, all co-owners will want to sign the revocation. If you own the property with someone else and you all have the right of survivorship, the revocation isn't effective unless it's signed by the last surviving owner.

Example: *Joyce and Eric own their house in tenancy by the entirety, which gives each of them the right of survivorship. They sign and record a T.O.D. deed leaving the house to their daughter. Later, Joyce records a revocation. If she dies first, Eric will be the sole owner. Because he didn't sign the revocation, it will have no effect, and their daughter will own the property when Eric dies.*

SAMPLE REVOCATION OF TRANSFER-ON-DEATH DEED (ARKANSAS)

REVOCATION OF BENEFICIARY DEED
CAUTION: THIS REVOCATION MUST BE RECORDED PRIOR TO
THE DEATH OF THE GRANTOR IN ORDER TO BE EFFECTIVE.

The undersigned hereby revokes the beneficiary deed recorded on July
19, 20xx, instrument number 3388449, records of Lane County,
Arkansas.
    Date: <u>September 4, 20xx</u>
    Signature of grantor(s): <u>Marilee N. Simmons</u>

[Notarization]

---

2. Record a New T.O.D. Deed

You can also simply sign and record a new T.O.D. deed, leaving the
property to someone else. Most states' laws specifically say that if there is
more than one T.O.D. deed, only the most recent one is valid. It's still
clearer, however, to record a revocation and then a new deed.

3. Transfer the Property to Someone Else

You are free to give away or sell the property that you've left in a T.O.D.
deed. If you no longer own the property at your death, the T.O.D. deed
will have no effect.

E. How the New Owner Claims the Property

After the real estate's owner dies, generally, all the T.O.D. beneficiary
has to do is file a short sworn statement (affidavit) and the death certifi-

cate in the public land records. This establishes a record of when the property changed hands and who the new owner is.

In most states, the affidavit must state the name of the new owner, describe the property, and give the date of the previous owner's death. It may also have to state the value of the property at the date of death. A sample affidavit, from Nevada, is shown below. Remember, however, that the T.O.D. beneficiary should check the state statute or consult a lawyer to find out the exact requirements in effect when the transfer takes place.

SAMPLE DEATH OF GRANTOR AFFIDAVIT (NEVADA)

DEATH OF GRANTOR AFFIDAVIT

Madison R. Benjamin, being duly sworn, deposes and says that Julius M. Benjamin, the decedent mentioned in the attached certified copy of the Certificate of Death, is the same person as Julius M. Benjamin, named as the grantor or as one of the grantors in the deed recorded on March 13, 20xx, instrument number 9929990, records of Washoe County, Nevada, covering the following described property:

[Legal description]

Madison R. Benjamin is the grantee or at least one of the grantees to whom the real property is conveyed upon the death of the grantor Julius M. Benjamin or is the authorized representative of the grantee or at least one of the grantees.

   February 12, 20xx   *Madison R. Benjamin*

(Date)   (Signature)

[notarization]

CHAPTER 6

Hold Property in Joint Ownership

If you own valuable property with someone else, you may already have a leg up in the probate-avoidance climb. Several forms of joint ownership—joint tenancy, for example—allow you to avoid probate when the first owner dies.

Many couples conclude that holding title to their major assets in a form of joint ownership that avoids probate is all the estate planning they want to engage in, at least while they are younger. The most attractive features of this strategy are its simplicity and economy. To take title with someone else in a way that will avoid probate, you usually don't have to prepare any additional documents. All you do is state, on the paper that shows your ownership (a real estate deed, for example), how you want to hold title. No expense, no lawyers.

When one owner dies, it's easy for the survivor to transfer the property into his or her name alone, without probate. After that, however, the survivor will have to find another method to avoid probate on his or her death.

A. Kinds of Joint Ownership That Avoid Probate

There are several ways to own property together with someone else, and it's important to realize that not all of these ways avoid probate. The most common forms of co-ownership are listed below. Scan the list to see which of the probate-avoidance options may be available to you; each one is discussed in detail later in the chapter.

JOINT OWNERSHIP METHODS

Method of Holding Title	Avoids Probate?
Joint tenancy with right of survivorship	Yes
Tenancy by the entirety*	Yes
Community property* (Alaska, Arizona, California, Idaho, Louisiana, Nevada, New Mexico, Texas, Washington, Wisconsin)	No, except in states where right of survivorship can be added
Community property with right of survivorship* (Alaska, Arizona, California, Nevada, Wisconsin)	Yes
Tenancy in common	No
Partnership	No

*Married couples only (or in some states, registered domestic partners); not available in all states.

You and your mate may already own your house, joint bank accounts, or other valuable property in a way that will avoid probate when one of you dies. When title and escrow companies prepare real estate deeds, it's a common practice for them to list the new owners as joint tenants or, if they're married, as tenants by the entirety, unless you direct otherwise.

Not sure just how you hold title? You're not alone. Most people don't pay much attention to how their names are listed on title documents. Fortunately, usually all it takes is a glance at those documents—for example, the deed to your house—to see how you and the other co-owner currently hold title.

IF YOU'RE NOT SURE HOW YOU HOLD TITLE

Kind of Property	Where to Look
Real estate	Your deed
Bank account	The passbook, or the registration card on file at the bank
Brokerage account	A statement for the account
Car, boat, or other vehicle	Certificate of ownership (title) or registration slip
Individual stocks or bonds	Stock certificates or bonds

B. Joint Tenancy

Joint tenancy is unquestionably the most popular probate-avoidance device around. And why not? Property owned in joint tenancy automatically passes, without probate, to the surviving owner(s) when one owner dies. Setting up a joint tenancy is easy, and it doesn't cost a penny.

Joint tenancy often works well when couples (married or not) acquire real estate, vehicles, bank accounts, securities, or other valuable property together. There can be, however, some serious drawbacks (discussed below), especially if you own property by yourself and are thinking of making someone else a joint tenant just to avoid probate.

In many states, married couples often take title not in joint tenancy, but in "tenancy by the entirety" instead. It's very similar to joint tenancy, but is limited to married couples only. (In Hawaii, New Jersey, and Vermont, however, registered domestic partners can also own property as tenants by the entirety.) Both avoid probate in exactly the same way.

(If you're married and interested in tenancy by the entirety, read this section first for the general joint tenancy rules; then check Section C, below, which discusses the special characteristics of tenancy by the entirety.)

JOINT TENANCY AT A GLANCE

Pros

- It's easy to create.
- It's easy for the survivor to transfer title to himself or herself after one owner dies.
- It works for just about anything you own: cars, real estate, bank accounts, stocks, and more.
- The survivor doesn't have to worry about creditors' claims. After one owner dies, joint tenancy property is subject only to claims for debts that are the joint responsibility of both joint tenants.
- You can have two or more joint tenants, as long as each owns an equal share.

Cons

- The last surviving joint tenant must use another method to avoid probate at his or her death.
- Probate is not avoided if both owners die simultaneously (a very unlikely event).
- Shares of each owner must be equal (except in Vermont).
- Not available for some kinds of property in some states.
- If you own property by yourself, adding a joint tenant requires making a gift of a half-interest in the property.

1. How Joint Tenancy Avoids Probate

When one joint owner (called a joint tenant, though it has nothing to do with renting) dies, the surviving joint owners automatically get the deceased owner's share of the joint tenancy property. This automatic transfer to the survivors is called the "right of survivorship." The property doesn't go through probate court—the survivor(s) need only shuffle some simple paperwork to get the property into their names.

The exact steps depend on the type of property, but generally all the new owner has to do is fill out a straightforward form and present it, with a death certificate, to the keeper of ownership records: a bank, state motor vehicles department, or county real estate records office.

Example: *Evelyn and her daughter Miya own a car together, registered in their names as joint tenants with right of survivorship. When Evelyn dies, her half-interest in the car will go to her daughter without probate. To get the car registered in her name alone, Miya will need only to fill out a simple form and file it with the state motor vehicles agency.*

If you're a joint tenant, you cannot leave your share to anyone other than the surviving joint tenants. So even if your will specifically leaves your half-interest in a joint tenancy car or house to someone else, the will has no effect. The surviving joint tenant will automatically own the property after your death.

But this rule is less ironclad than it may sound. A joint tenant can easily, and unilaterally, break the joint tenancy at any time before death.

Example: *Eleanor and Sadie own a house together as joint tenants. Without telling Sadie, Eleanor signs a deed (and records it in the county land records office) transferring her half-interest from herself as a joint tenant to herself as a "tenant in common." (Tenancy in common is a form of co-ownership that does not include the right of survivorship.) This ends the joint tenancy, leaving Eleanor free to leave her half-interest in the property to someone else in her will.*

In theory, you could also end a joint tenancy by transferring your share of the property to someone else. But this is unlikely, because very few outsiders want to buy into a co-ownership with a stranger. You could, however, give your share to someone, or a creditor may go after it. If a joint tenant does transfer a share of property to a new owner, that new owner isn't a joint tenant with the other original owners. Instead, they are "tenants in common," a form of ownership that does not carry with it the right of survivorship.

Example 1: *Sean and Alice own a beach house, which they inherited from their parents, in joint tenancy. Sean gives his half-interest to his grown children, making them tenants in common with Alice. When Alice dies, her interest will not automatically go to Sean's children. Instead, it will pass under the terms of her will.*

Example 2: *Don, Melanie, and Barbara own property together in joint tenancy. Don deeds his one-third interest to Josh, his son. Josh is not a joint tenant with Melanie and Barbara; he is a tenant in common, free to leave his property to whomever he wants. Melanie and Barbara, however, are still joint tenants with respect to their two-thirds of the property; when one of them dies, the other will own a two-thirds share.*

2. Limitations of Joint Tenancy

There are definite limits on the effectiveness of joint ownership as a probate-avoidance strategy. Most of these drawbacks are of greatest concern to older folks.

Probate is not avoided when the last owner dies. One drawback is obvious: The probate-avoidance part of joint tenancy works only at the death of the first co-owner. (Or, if there are three joint tenants, only at the death of the first two, and so on.) When the last co-owner dies, the property must go through probate before it goes to whomever inherits it, unless the last owner used a different probate-avoidance method, such as transferring the property to a living trust. By contrast, some other probate-avoidance devices, such as living trusts or payable-on-death accounts, let you name a beneficiary who will inherit free of probate when the second co-owner dies.

Probate is not avoided if both owners die simultaneously. In that very unlikely event, each owner's share of the property would pass under the terms of his or her will. If a joint tenant died without a valid will, the property would go to each owner's closest relatives under state law. Either way, probate would probably be necessary.

Don't obsess about simultaneous death. Nolo gets a lot of questions about what happens to joint tenancy property if both members of a couple die in a common disaster. It's a natural concern, but one that shouldn't loom large in your estate planning. Statistically, the chances are almost negligible that co-owners will die at the same time.

One owner's incapacity may hobble the others. Another issue that may concern elderly or ill persons is that if one joint owner became incapacitated and could not make decisions, the other owners' freedom to act would be restricted. This problem can be avoided if each joint owner signs a document called a "Durable Power of Attorney," giving someone authority to manage their affairs if they cannot, or if the property is transferred to a living trust. (See Chapter 7 for information on living trusts.)

3. Drawbacks of Adding a New Joint Tenant Just to Avoid Probate

Joint tenancy is usually a poor estate planning choice when an older person, seeking only to avoid probate, is tempted to put solely owned property into joint tenancy with someone else. Adding another owner this way creates several potential headaches.

You're giving away property. If you make someone else a joint tenant of property that you now own yourself, you give up half owner-ship of the property. The new owner could sell or mortgage his or her share—or lose it to creditors.

Example: *An Arizona woman and her adult son took title to a condominium as joint tenants. The mother, who had owned the condo with her daughter until then, paid all expenses of the property and received all the income from renting it to tenants.*

Later the IRS sued the son for unpaid income taxes, and eventually the condominium was sold to pay the taxes. The mother received half of the proceeds. She sued to get the other half back, arguing that she was the only true owner because the joint tenancy had been created only for estate planning purposes. She lost. If you put property into joint tenancy, the IRS presumes you intend to make a gift, and she could not overcome that legal presumption. (Nikirk v. U.S., 2003 WL 22474742 (D. Ariz. 2003).)

GIFT AND ESTATE TAXES

If you create a joint tenancy by making another person a co-owner, federal gift tax may be assessed on the transfer. If gifts to one person (except your spouse) in one year exceed the federal gift tax exclusion (currently $12,000), you must file a gift tax return with the IRS. No tax is actually due, however, until you give away more than the amount of the estate tax threshold in taxable gifts. (See Chapter 9.)

There's one big exception: If two or more people own a bank account in joint tenancy, but one person puts all or most of the money in, no gift tax is assessed against that person. The theory is that because the contributor still has the power to withdraw the money, no gift has been made yet. A taxable gift may be made, however, when the other joint tenant withdraws money from it. (IRS Priv. Ltr. Rul. 94-27003, 1994.)

For federal estate tax purposes, however, you are treated as if you had not given away a part interest in the property. The entire joint tenancy property remains in your taxable estate—the property which, at your death, is subject to federal estate tax. (Most estates don't have to pay estate tax, however, because such a large amount of property is exempt from the tax.) This rule has another consequence as well: At your death, the new owner (the surviving joint tenant) gets a tax basis that is "stepped-up" to the date-of-death value. This can be a valuable tax break for the survivor.

It may spawn disputes after your death. Many older people make the mistake of adding someone as a joint tenant to a bank account just for "convenience." They want someone to help them out by depositing checks and paying bills. But after the original owner dies, the co-owner may claim that he or she is entitled, as a surviving joint tenant, to keep the funds remaining in the account. In some instances, maybe that's what the deceased person really intended—it's too late to ask. Sadly, this sort of confusion often leads to bitter and permanent family rifts, some of which are fought out in court.

I REMEMBER MAMA, AND HER MONEY

A Georgia lawsuit pitted one woman against her siblings, squabbling over their deceased mother's certificates of deposit. The daughter's name had been added to the certificates as a joint owner, and after her mother's death she claimed the money belonged to her.

But the other offspring recalled—and testified at the trial—that the daughter had been the one who suggested the joint-owner arrangement, purportedly to make the money readily available "in case Mama got sick." The jury decided that the joint tenancy had been for convenience only, and that the mother had not intended to make a gift to the daughter. (*Turner v. Mikell,* 195 Ga. App. 766, 395 S.E.2d 20 (1990).)

Other ways to accomplish your goal. If you just want someone to write checks for you, there are far better ways to do it. If you merely want someone to deposit and write checks for you, consider giving a trusted person a "power of attorney." When you sign a power of attorney, the person you choose, known as your "attorney-in-fact," can act on your behalf—but has no right to the funds in the account. Many banks have their own forms you can use to give someone this limited authority. It's easy to establish or revoke; you don't need a lawyer.

A few states now offer the useful option of a "convenience" account. Florida, for example, lets a depositor name one or more "agents" who have the right to make deposits, withdraw funds, and write checks on the depositor's behalf. An agent has no rights to the money and doesn't inherit it when the depositor dies.

A surviving spouse may miss an income tax break. If you make your spouse a joint tenant with you on property you own separately, the surviving spouse could miss out on a potentially big income tax break later, when the property is sold.

You need concern yourself with this problem only if:

- you own property separately and want to make your spouse a joint tenant now instead of leaving the property to him or her at your death,

- the property's value has gone up (or you expect it to)—something that may happen to real estate or stocks, but not other common property like cars or household goods, and

- you *don't* live in a community property state (Arizona, California, Idaho, Louisiana, Nevada, New Mexico, Texas, Washington, or Wisconsin).

To understand the problem, you need to know a little about IRS "tax basis" rules. The tax basis on any item of property is the amount from which taxable profit is figured when property is sold. Usually, basis is what you paid for the property, with some adjustments. For example, if you buy an antique for $100, that amount is your basis. If, 20 years later, you sell it for $400, IRS rules let you subtract your $100 basis, leaving $300 in taxable profit.

If you own a piece of property by yourself and leave it to your spouse at your death, his or her tax basis is the market value of the property at the time it's inherited. If the value of the property has gone up, the basis goes up (it's "stepped up," in tax jargon), too. That's good, because a higher basis means lower taxable profit when the property is sold.

By contrast, if you transfer the solely owned property to joint tenancy with your spouse, the tax basis of the half you give stays exactly the same; it isn't stepped up. (26 U.S.C. § 2040.)

As noted above, there's a special rule for couples in community property states: Both halves of community property get a stepped-up basis when one spouse dies. This is true even if the community property is held in joint tenancy. But in that case, the surviving spouse must show the IRS that the joint tenancy property was in fact community property—that is, that it was bought with community property funds. If the title documents say joint tenancy, that's what the IRS will go by. You may be better off holding title as community property in the first place; see Section D, below.

Federal legislation passed in 2001 restricts the availability of stepped-up basis for inherited property—but not until 2010.

4. How to Take Title in Joint Tenancy

Joint tenancy certainly has the virtue of simplicity. To create a joint tenancy, all you need to do is pay attention to the way you and the other co-owners are listed on the title document, such as a deed to real estate, a car's title slip, or the signature card establishing a bank account. In the great majority of states, by calling yourselves "joint tenants with the right of survivorship," or putting the abbreviation "JT WROS" after your names, you create a joint tenancy. (But in South Carolina, to hold real estate in joint tenancy, the deed should use the words "as joint tenants with rights of survivorship, and not as tenants in common," just to make it crystal clear. S.C. Code Ann. § 27-7-40.)

A car salesman or bank staffer may assure you that other words are enough. For example, connecting the names of the owners with the word "or," not "and," does create a joint tenancy, in some circumstances, in some states. But it's always better to unambiguously spell out what you want: joint tenancy with right of survivorship.

Example: *When Ken and his wife Janelle buy a house, they want to take title in joint tenancy. When the deed that transfers the house to them is prepared, all they need to do is tell the title company to identify them on it this way: "Kenneth J. Hartman and Janelle M. Grubcek as joint tenants with right of survivorship." There should be no extra cost or paperwork.*

Joint tenancy is available in all states, although a few impose restrictions, summarized below. Remember that one rule applies in every state except Vermont: All joint tenants must own equal shares of the property. If you want a different arrangement, such as 60-40 ownership, joint tenancy is not for you.

STATE RESTRICTIONS ON JOINT TENANCY

Alaska	No joint tenancy in real estate, except for husband and wife, who may own as tenants by the entirety
Oregon	Transfer to husband and wife creates tenancy by the entirety, not joint tenancy
Tennessee	Transfer to husband and wife creates tenancy by the entirety, not joint tenancy
Texas	To establish joint tenancy, owners must sign joint tenancy agreement
Wisconsin	No joint tenancy between spouses; property becomes survivorship marital property

⚠ **In Texas, you need a separate written agreement.** If you want to set up a joint tenancy in Texas, you and the other joint tenants must sign a written agreement. For example, if you want to create a joint tenancy bank account, so that the survivor will get all the funds, specifying your arrangement on the bank's signature card isn't enough. Fortunately, a bank or real estate office should be able to give you a fill-in-the-blanks form that will do the trick.

Take this requirement seriously. A dispute over such an account ended up in the Texas Supreme Court. Two sisters had set up an account together, using a signature card that allowed the survivor to withdraw the funds. But when one sister died, and the other withdrew the funds, the estate of the deceased sister sued—and won the funds—because there was no separate agreement in writing. (*Stauffer v. Henderson*, 801 S.W.2d 858 (Tex. 1991).)

C. Tenancy by the Entirety

Tenancy by the entirety is very much like joint tenancy, but it's just for married couples (and in Hawaii, New Jersey, and Vermont, same-sex partners who have registered with the state). It has almost the same advantages and disadvantages of joint tenancy and is most useful in the same situation: when a couple acquires property together. This form of ownership is available in the states listed below.

STATES WITH TENANCY BY THE ENTIRETY OWNERSHIP

Alaska*	Missouri
Arkansas	New Jersey
Delaware*	New York*
District of Columbia	North Carolina*
Florida	Ohio* (only if created before
Hawaii	April 4, 1985)
Illinois*	Oklahoma
Indiana*	Oregon*
Kentucky*	Pennsylvania
Maryland	Rhode Island*
Massachusetts	Tennessee
Michigan (joint tenancy of	Utah*
husband and wife is automatically	Vermont
a tenancy by the entirety)	Virginia
Mississippi	Wyoming

*for real estate only

TENANCY BY THE ENTIRETY AT A GLANCE

Pros

- It's easy to create.
- It's easy to transfer title to the spouse.
- Tenancy by the entirety property is usually subject only to claims for debts that are the joint responsibility of both spouses

Cons

- Probate is avoided only when the first spouse dies. The surviving survivor must use another method to avoid probate at his or her death.
- Probate is not avoided if the spouses die simultaneously (a very unlikely event).
- Each spouse must own a half-share.
- Not available in all states.
- In some states, limited to real estate.

There are a few important differences, however, between joint tenancy and tenancy by the entirety. For one, if property is held in tenancy by the entirety, neither spouse can transfer his or her half of the property alone, either while alive or by will or trust. It must go to the surviving spouse. This is different from joint tenancy; a joint tenant is free to break the joint tenancy at any time (see Section B, above).

Example: *Fred and Ethel hold title to their house in tenancy by the entirety. If Fred wanted to sell or give away his half-interest in the house, he could not do so without Ethel's signature on the deed.*

Other differences may also be important to you. In general, tenancy by the entirety property is better protected than joint tenancy property from creditors of just one spouse. If someone sues one spouse and wins a court judgment, in most states the creditor can't seize and sell tenancy by the entirety property to pay off the debt. And if one spouse files for bankruptcy, creditors can't reach or sever property held in tenancy by the entirety.

D. Community Property

If you are married and live in a community property state, another way to take title to property with your spouse is available to you: community property. In some states, community property doesn't have to go through probate; in others, it does. You'll have to take a look at your state's rules, discussed below, before you make up your mind about how to hold title. But in states where community property ownership furnishes both probate avoidance and tax benefits after one spouse dies, it may be a better choice than joint tenancy. Tenancy by the entirety is not available in community property states.

COMMUNITY PROPERTY STATES

Alaska*	Nevada
Arizona	New Mexico
California	Texas
Idaho	Washington
Louisiana	Wisconsin

*Only if spouses sign a community property agreement.

1. Community Property Basics

If you're married and live in a community property state, most property acquired by you or your spouse during the marriage is automatically community property, unless you sign an agreement to the contrary. Most important, your earnings are community property, and so is everything you buy with those earnings.

There are important exceptions: Property that one spouse inherits or receives as a gift is not community property. If, however, it gets so mixed with community property that it can no longer be separated—for example, money you inherit is deposited in a joint bank account from which you make withdrawals—it, too, becomes community property.

Each spouse owns a half-interest in the community property, and each has equal rights to use and manage it. The consent of both spouses, however, is usually required before the property can be sold or mortgaged.

The law does not require community property go to the surviving spouse when one spouse dies. Each spouse is free to leave his or her half-interest in the community property to someone else. (Spouses can change this by the way they hold title to the property, as discussed below.) If community property isn't left to the surviving spouse, probate isn't avoided.

A tax break for the survivor. Community property offers a tax break to the surviving spouse if the property has gone up in value before the first spouse's death. This benefit has to do with tax basis. As explained in Section B, above, the tax basis is the amount from which taxable profit is figured when property is sold; usually, it's what you paid for the property, with some adjustments.

If you hold property in joint tenancy with your spouse, at your death only the tax basis of your half of the property is stepped up to its market value at the time of death. The tax basis of the surviving spouse's half stays the same. When the property is later sold, this means higher tax if the property went up in value after the joint tenancy was created but before the first spouse died.

If you hold title to the same property as community property, however—or can prove to the IRS that property held in joint tenancy was actually community property—the tax basis for the whole property is stepped up when one spouse dies. (26 U.S.C. § 1014(b)(6).) That leads to a lower taxable profit if the property is later sold.

Example: *Hank and Beatrice own their house, which they bought many years ago for $60,000, in community property. When Beatrice dies, the house is worth $130,000. Hank inherits her half-interest; his tax basis goes up to $130,000.*

If Hank and Beatrice had owned the property in joint tenancy and Hank could not prove to the IRS that it was community property, held in joint tenancy for convenience, his tax basis would be just $95,000 (the $30,000 basis in his half plus the $65,000 basis in her half).

Joint tenants may not be out of luck. If the surviving spouse can prove to the IRS that the joint tenancy property was actually community property, held in joint tenancy for convenience, he or she can qualify for the favorable tax treatment.

2. Community Property With the Right of Survivorship

If you live in one of the community property states listed below, you may want to take advantage of an option that lets you avoid probate completely for community property. Those states let couples hold title to property as "community property with right of survivorship" —meaning that when one spouse dies, the other automatically owns the community property.

STATES WHERE YOU CAN HOLD TITLE AS COMMUNITY PROPERTY WITH RIGHT OF SURVIVORSHIP

Alaska
Arizona
California
Nevada
Wisconsin

COMMUNITY PROPERTY WITH RIGHT OF SURVIVORSHIP AT A GLANCE

Pros

- It's easy to hold title this way.
- It's easy to transfer title to the surviving spouse.
- It works for anything a married couple owns: cars, real estate, bank accounts, stocks, and more.
- If property goes up in value, the surviving spouse gets an income tax break (compared to holding it in joint tenancy) when the property is sold.

Cons

- The surviving spouse must use another method to avoid probate at his or her death (except in Wisconsin; see below).
- Probate is not avoided if both spouses die simultaneously (a very unlikely event).

If you hold title this way, the process of transferring title to the surviving spouse is as simple as transferring joint tenancy property. The exact steps depend on the type of property, but generally all the new owner has to do is fill out a straightforward form and present it, with a death certificate, to the keeper of ownership records: a bank, state motor vehicles department, or county real estate records office.

Example: *Michael and Marla, who live in Nevada, took title to their house as "community property with right of survivorship." After Michael dies, Marla takes his death certificate to the office of the county registrar of deeds. She fills out and files the form provided by that office, which asks her for some basic information about her late husband and the property. When the form is recorded (filed) by the registrar of deeds, it's as good as a probate court order would be as proof that Marla now owns the property.*

To turn plain community (or separate) property into right-of-survivorship community property, you simply need to put the right words on the title document, just as you would for joint tenancy property.

ADDING THE RIGHT OF SURVIVORSHIP TO COMMUNITY PROPERTY

State	Procedure	Statute
Alaska	Couples take title to property as "survivorship community property."	Alaska Stat. § 34.77.110(e)
Arizona	Couples take title to specific property as "community property with right of survivorship."	Ariz. Rev. Stat. § 33-431
California	Couples take title to specific property as "community property with right of survivorship."	Cal. Civ. Code § 682.1
Nevada	Couples take title to specific property as "community property with right of survivorship."	Nev. Rev. Stat. § 111.064
Wisconsin	Couples take title to specific property as "survivorship marital property" or sign a marital property agreement (see Section 3, below).	Wis. Stat. Ann. §§ 766.58, 766.60

Spouses are free to change their minds and remove the survivorship provision later, but it must be done in writing. They should prepare a new title document that does not include the right of survivorship.

Example: *When Liz and her husband Fernando bought their vacation house, they directed the title company to state, on the deed to the property, that they would own it as community property with right of survivorship.*

Years later, they decide that they want Fernando's son, Robert, to inherit his father's half-interest in the house. Liz and Fernando sign and record a new deed, changing the way they hold property to plain "community property." In his will, Fernando leaves his half-interest to Robert.

A spouse may also be able to act alone to revoke a right of survivorship. In Nevada, a spouse can wipe out the right of survivorship by transferring his or her half-interest in the property. And in Arizona, to remove the right of survivorship from a piece of real estate, either spouse can file a sworn statement, called an "affidavit terminating right of survivorship," with the county recorder in the county where the real estate is located. The state statute sets out what information the affidavit must contain.

3. Community Property Agreements

In Alaska, Idaho, Texas, Washington, and Wisconsin, a married couple can sign an agreement that will determine what happens to some or all of their property at death. Usually, couples declare all of their property to be community property and leave it to the survivor, without probate, when one spouse dies. In effect, the agreement functions much like a will—with the important difference that the property doesn't have to go through probate when the first spouse dies.

STATES THAT AUTHORIZE COMMUNITY PROPERTY AGREEMENTS

State	Statute
Alaska	Alaska Stat. § 34.77.090
Idaho	Idaho Code § 15-6-201
Texas	Tex. Probate Code Ann. § 451
Washington	Wash. Rev. Code § 26.16.120
Wisconsin	Wis. Stat. Ann. § 766.58

Different states have different rules about what makes community property agreements valid. All states require them to be in writing. They may need to be witnessed or notarized. You may also need to record (file) them in the county where you live and where any real estate that's covered is located.

Be sure you understand what you're doing. If you want to create a community property agreement, be sure to check your state's current rules. If you don't, your agreement may not have the effect you intend.

Another reason for caution is that these agreements are binding contracts. Neither spouse can, acting alone, change or revoke them. To revoke a community property agreement, generally the spouses must:

- agree to cancel (rescind) the agreement
- divorce, or
- separate permanently.

If you and your spouse later run into marital trouble, the agreement will remain in effect unless you agree to revoke it or you get a divorce. Just making a will that leaves your property in a different way may not revoke the agreement.

Example: *Angeline and her husband John, who lived in Washington, signed a community property agreement declaring that when one of them died, everything the deceased spouse owned would be converted to community property and would go to the survivor. Later, Angeline and John separated. John filed for legal separation. Angeline made a new will, leaving nothing to John, and died two days later.*

A legal fight ensued, with John claiming that the agreement was still valid and so he was entitled to inherit all of Angeline's property. A state appeals court ruled that it would read into the community property agreement a clause that wasn't there but that the spouses would surely have wanted: namely, that the agreement would end if the spouses separated permanently. (In re Bachmeier, *106 Wash. App. 862, 25 P.3d 498 (2001).*)

Just a few years earlier, the same court had ruled that, under very similar circumstances, a community property agreement was *not* revoked. (*In re Estate of Catto*, 88 Wash. App. 522, 944 P.2d 1052 (1997), rev. denied, 134 Wash. 2d 1017, 958 P.2d 313 (1998).)

Questions? See a lawyer. These rules are mostly determined by courts, and may change. If you have questions about the validity of a community property agreement, or want to revoke one, see a lawyer.

In Alaska and Wisconsin, a community property agreement can name a beneficiary to inherit the property at the *second* spouse's death. (In Washington, there is confusion about whether or not spouses can do this. Some commentators say that it's allowed, but courts have not explicitly said so.) After one spouse dies, however, the survivor can amend the agreement to change who inherits his or her property, unless the agreement expressly forbids it.

Example: *Julie and Alphonse make a community property agreement. The agreement states that when one of them dies, all of his or her property will go to the surviving spouse. The agreement further states that when the second spouse dies, everything he or she owns will go to Julie's son from a prior marriage.*

Julie dies first. Alphonse decides that he doesn't want to leave everything to Julie's son; he wants to leave some money to charity at his death as well. He is free to do so.

4. Regular Community Property

Of the other community property states, California is the only one to offer significant probate-avoidance for community property that isn't held with the right of survivorship.

California allows regular community property to pass outside of probate, via two different procedures. For real estate, the spouse simply files a one-page affidavit (sworn statement) with the county recorder's office. The affidavit states that he or she is entitled to full ownership of the property. For other property, the spouse requests a Spousal Property Order from the probate court, which then authorizes the transfer into the surviving spouse's name.

Idaho offers a simple probate procedure when the surviving spouse didn't leave a will, the entire estate is community property, and the surviving spouse is the only heir. The surviving spouse files a simple petition with the probate court, and the court issues an order stating that the survivor now owns everything.

New Mexico allows a surviving spouse to take title to a home held in community property without probate. But there are several limitations: It's allowed only after a six-month waiting period, only if probate isn't necessary for any other assets, and only if all debts and taxes have been paid.

Washington offers no probate shortcuts for community property. Unless you've signed a community property agreement, community property goes through probate just like everything else.

REGULAR COMMUNITY PROPERTY (NO RIGHT OF SURVIVORSHIP) AT A GLANCE

Pros

- It's easy to create.
- It can apply to anything a couple owns: cars, real estate, bank accounts, stocks, and more.
- If property goes up in value, surviving spouse gets an income tax break (compared to holding it in joint tenancy) when the property is sold.

Cons

- NO PROBATE AVOIDANCE except in California.
- Even in California, the surviving spouse must use another method to avoid probate at his or her death, and probate is not avoided if both spouses die simultaneously (a very unlikely event).

Obviously, if you live outside California, holding assets as plain community property (no right of survivorship) doesn't do anything to advance your probate-avoidance planning. For this reason, you may want to hold title to your community property as joint tenancy or put it in a living trust. The property is still, legally, community property, but when one spouse dies, it can be passed to the survivor without probate.

Example: *Marielle and Arnold live in Washington state. When they buy a house with community property funds (money from their joint bank account), they decide to create a living trust and transfer the house to it. So on the deed that gives them ownership of the property, they list themselves as "Marielle and Arnold Bruchman, trustees of the Marielle and Arnold Bruchman Revocable Living Trust dated January 31, 20xx."*

The house will still be community property, subject to all state community property laws. But when Marielle or Arnold dies, the survivor will be able to transfer the house without probate.

E. Alternatives to Joint Ownership

If you think that joint ownership isn't for you, you may be casting about for another probate-avoidance method. This book, of course, is full of alternatives. Here are some for a few kinds of assets commonly placed in joint tenancy.

Payable-on-death designations for bank accounts or securities. Adding a beneficiary designation is a simple, free way to avoid probate. See Chapter 1, which discusses payable-on-death bank accounts, and Chapter 3, which explains how to name a beneficiary for securities.

Living trusts for real estate. A living trust is the most flexible alternative for real estate. A trust, unlike joint ownership, allows you to name a beneficiary to inherit the property if the other co-owner dies before you do. And if you transfer the property to a living trust, you will avoid probate both when the first owner dies and when the second one dies. With joint ownership, of course, probate is avoided only when the first owner dies.

Transfer-on-Death Deeds for Real Estate. In several states, you can transfer real estate without probate by preparing a deed now that takes effect only at your death. See Chapter 5

■

CHAPTER 7

Create a Living Trust

You've probably heard of living trusts, which are also called revocable living trusts or (by lawyers) "inter vivos" trusts. Perhaps you've even been advised—by a lawyer, a newspaper columnist, or your Uncle Harry—that you ought to have one. But if you're like most people, you still have some basic questions: What, exactly, is a living trust? How does it work? And do I really need one?

Living trusts (they're called that just because you create them while you're alive, not in your will) were invented to let people make an end-run around probate. Holding your valuable property in trust has virtually no legal consequences while you're alive, because you control the

REVOCABLE LIVING TRUSTS AT A GLANCE

Pros

- A trust works for anything you own: cars, real estate, bank accounts, stocks, and more.
- You can name alternate beneficiaries (unlike many probate-avoidance techniques).
- You can amend or revoke the trust at any time.
- There is no waiting period after death; property can be transferred to beneficiaries quickly.
- A trust is harder to attack in court than a will.
- Spouses can make one combined trust.
- If you become incapacitated, the successor trustee can take over management of trust property without court authorization.

Cons

- A trust is more work to create and maintain than other probate-avoidance devices, because property must be transferred, in writing, to the trustee.
- You may run into hassles if you want to refinance property owned by the trust.
- It's unlikely, but in some places you might have to pay a transfer tax if you put real estate in the trust.

trust. (And you can end it at any time, if you choose to.) But after your death, property held in trust can be easily transferred to the family or friends you left it to—without probate. The terms of the trust document (which is similar to a will) authorize the trustee to make this transfer. Probate courts have no legal authority over property that's held in trust.

As you can see, a living trust performs much the same function as a will. The crucial difference is that property left through a will must go through probate, while property in a living trust can go directly to your inheritors.

A. How a Living Trust Avoids Probate

A trust can seem like a mysterious creature, dreamed up by lawyers, wrapped in legal jargon, and used for mysterious purposes. But in practice, a standard probate-avoidance trust isn't complicated. Here are the basics.

1. Trust Basics

The kind of trust that avoids probate is called a revocable living trust. You can create one simply by preparing and signing a document called a Declaration (or Instrument) of Trust. If you and your spouse own valuable property together, you'll probably want to create one trust, together.

The trust document, much like a will, names the people or institutions you want to inherit each item of trust property. One significant advantage of a living trust over simpler probate-avoidance methods is that you can name alternate beneficiaries—people who will inherit if your first choice does not survive you. You can even name alternates for your alternates, if you want an extra layer of contingency planning.

Once you've signed the trust document, you transfer your property—real estate, stocks, bank accounts, whatever—to the trustee, who becomes the legal owner. This step is crucial. If you don't transfer ownership, in writing, to the trustee, the trust document has no effect on what happens to the property at your death.

Holding property in trust has almost no day-to-day effect while you're alive. For all practical purposes, it's as if you still owned it. The property is treated the same way it was before by the government when it assesses income or estate taxes, and by creditors when they are looking to collect on a debt you owe.

2. Who's in Charge

The trustee is in charge of trust property. You (or you and your spouse, if you create a trust together) are the trustee of your revocable living trust, which means that you keep complete control of all the trust property. As trustee, you can transfer property in and out of the trust, change the beneficiaries you've named, or revoke the trust completely.

Example: *Ashley Zallon creates a living trust, the Ashley Zallon Revocable Living Trust, and transfers her valuable property—a house and some stocks—into the trust. She names herself as trustee of the trust. As trustee, she can sell, mortgage, or give away the trust property, or take it out of the trust and put it back into her name.*

You can refinance a mortgage, even if your bank is grumpy about it. Living trusts are so common these days that banks shouldn't raise an eyebrow if you want to refinance property that's legally held in your name as a trustee instead of as an individual. If your bank or title company does ask questions, it should be reassured if you present a copy of your trust document, which should specifically give you, as trustee, the power to borrow against trust property.

In the unlikely event you can't convince a lender to deal with you in your capacity as trustee, find another lender or transfer the property out of the trust and back into your name. Later, after you refinance, you can transfer it back into the living trust.

3. How Property Is Transferred After Your Death

After you die, the person you named in your trust document to be the "successor trustee" takes over as trustee. He or she is in charge of transferring the trust property to the family, friends, or charities you named as the trust beneficiaries. In most cases, the whole transfer process can be handled within a few weeks at little or no cost.

No probate is necessary for property that was held in trust. For example, if you left real estate in your trust to your son Paul, the successor trustee can simply sign a deed transferring the property from the trust to Paul.

With property like bank accounts or securities, the successor trustee will need to show the institution that he or she has the legal right to take possession of the property. Banks and brokers, which have long experience with living trusts, generally accept the authority of the successor trustee without a fuss after examining a copy of the trust document, with its notarized signature.

Occasionally, however, an institution balks at the idea of releasing a deceased client's money without further proof of authority. It might, for example, demand more proof that the trust is valid or that it hasn't been revoked. In a few instances, institutions have threatened to withhold trust funds until they were shown a "certification" of validity by the lawyer or bank involved in drawing up the trust—even if that was impossible because no lawyer or bank had been involved.

No law requires that a lawyer, broker, or bank be involved with a living trust in any capacity. Requiring the signature of a lawyer or bank is simply a bureaucratic rule, imposed by financial institutions afraid of liability for turning over money to the wrong person. So shaking the money loose will not be an insurmountable problem, even if no lawyer drafted the trust. The successor trustee must simply be persistent. The bank should relent if the successor trustee produces the original, signed and notarized trust document, and offers his or her own notarized statement, stating that the trust is in full force and effect.

When all the trust property has been transferred to the beneficiaries, the living trust ceases to exist.

If you leave property to youngsters, you may want a living trust to continue after your death. You can arrange for your living trust to stay in existence for a while—even years—after your death. One common reason for doing this is so that property inherited by young beneficiaries can stay in trust, managed by an adult, until they're old enough to handle it on their own.

For example, say you're a divorced parent, and you want to leave trust property to your young daughter. You can direct, in your trust document, that if she is younger than 25 at your death, the property is to stay in trust and be managed for her by your successor trustee. When she turns 25, she will receive what's left, and the trust will end.

TRUSTS AND ESTATE TAXES

Like other probate-avoidance devices, a basic living trust has no effect on estate taxes. The taxing authorities don't care whether or not your property goes through probate; all they care about is what you owned at your death. Property you leave in a revocable living trust is still considered part of your estate for federal estate tax purposes.

There are, however, many other kinds of trusts that can save wealthy people money on federal estate taxes. The most common kind of tax-saving trust is the "credit shelter trust" or "AB trust," which is for couples. It works like this: A couple makes a trust together and transfers property to it. When the first spouse dies, his trust property goes to the children— with the crucial restriction that the surviving spouse has the right to use the income from that property for the rest of her life. When she dies, the trust ends, and the property goes to the children outright.

AB trusts generally make sense only for older, wealthier couples. Younger ones want the surviving spouse to have access to the trust property itself, not just the income. (For a thorough discussion of AB trusts, and forms and instructions for preparing one, see *Make Your Own Living Trust,* by Denis Clifford or *Quicken WillMaker Plus* software (both published by Nolo.)

B. Other Advantages of a Living Trust

As you know, the main reason for setting up a revocable living trust is to save your family time and money by avoiding probate. But there are other advantages as well.

1. Protection From Court Challenges

Court challenges to living trusts, like challenges to wills, are rare. But if there is a lawsuit, it's generally considered more difficult to successfully attack a living trust than a will. That's because your continuing involvement with a living trust after its creation (transferring property in and out of the trust, or making amendments) is evidence that you were competent to manage your affairs.

Someone who wanted to challenge the validity of your living trust would have to bring a lawsuit and prove that:

- when you made the trust, you were mentally incompetent or unduly influenced by someone, or
- the trust document itself is flawed—for example, because the signature was forged.

You needn't concern yourself with the possibility of a lawsuit at all unless you think that a close relative—someone who would inherit from you if you hadn't made the trust or will that you did—might have an ax to grind after your death. Pay attention to certain kinds of simmering family tensions, which sometimes boil over into lawsuits. Here are a few red flags:

- You have children from a previous marriage who don't get along with your current spouse, and either your spouse or the children might feel slighted.
- You are in a relationship—for example, with a gay or lesbian partner—that your closest relatives don't approve of.
- You have a history of mental illness, which might lead relatives to conclude you weren't thinking clearly when you made your trust.
- You don't plan to leave much property to close relatives, and they fear you are being unduly influenced by someone.

⚠ **See a lawyer if you fear a court battle after your death.** If you think relatives might try to turn your estate plan topsy-turvy after your death, talk to an experienced lawyer about how you can bolster your defenses.

2. Avoiding a Conservatorship

Having a living trust can be extremely useful if you someday become incapable, because of physical or mental illness, of taking care of your financial affairs. This is because if you've made a trust with your spouse or partner, he or she has authority over all the trust property. And if you've made an individual trust, your trust document probably authorizes your successor trustee, whose normal job is to take over as trustee at your death, to step in and manage trust property if you become incapacitated.

This feature of a living trust can be a godsend to family members who are distraught, or quite possibly overwhelmed, by caring for someone who has been struck by a serious illness or accident. Without the authority conferred in a living trust document, family members must usually go to court to get legal authority over the incapacitated person's finances—a painful, public process. Typically, the spouse or adult child of the person asks the court to be appointed as that person's conservator or guardian.

Most trust documents require that before a successor trustee can take charge of trust property, your incapacity would have to be certified in writing by one or two physicians. Once that determination has been properly made, the successor trustee has legal authority to manage all property in the trust, and to use it for your health care, support, and welfare. The law requires him or her to act honestly and prudently.

Example: *Margaret creates a revocable living trust, appointing herself as trustee. The trust document states that if she becomes incapacitated, and a physician signs a statement saying she no longer can manage her own affairs, her daughter Elizabeth will replace her as trustee. Elizabeth will be responsible for managing trust property and using it for her mother's benefit. At Margaret's death, Elizabeth will distribute the trust property according to the directions in the trust document.*

A successor trustee who takes over must also file an annual income tax return for the trust. (As long as you are the trustee of your own trust, no separate trust income tax return is required.)

You should also make a Durable Power of Attorney. Your successor trustee has no authority to manage property outside the trust. And because everyone has, at one time or another, some property that isn't owned by their living trust, it's always a good idea to prepare and sign a document called a Durable Power of Attorney for Financial Management. In this document, you can authorize your successor trustee to make financial and property management decisions for non-trust property if you become incapacitated.

In addition, if you are concerned about making sure doctors know your wishes about the use of various life-sustaining treatments—not being kept alive artificially, for example—you'll want to prepare and sign some other documents, commonly called a Directive to Physicians (living will) and Durable Power of Attorney for Health Care.

Making the Douments. *Quicken WillMaker Plus* software (published by Nolo) creates health care directives and power of attorney forms for every state, and financial durable power of attorney forms.

C. Why You Still Need a Will

A living trust, powerful as it is, doesn't eliminate the need for a will. There are two main reasons.

One big reason is that a living trust covers only property you have transferred, in writing, to the trust—and almost no one transfers everything to a trust. And even if you do scrupulously try to transfer everything, there's always the chance you'll acquire property shortly before you die. If you don't think to (or aren't able to) transfer ownership of it to your living trust, it won't pass under the terms of the trust document.

Second, a will can do some important things that a living trust document cannot. For example, in many states you must use a will if you have minor children and want to name a guardian—someone to raise them if you and the other parent die before they reach adulthood—for them. You can also use a will to forgive (cancel) debts owed to you, something that isn't done in a trust document.

If you use a living trust as your primary way to leave property, all you need is a bare-bones will. In it, state who should inherit any property that you don't specifically transfer to your living trust or leave to someone in some other way.

One kind of simple will is called a pour-over will, so named because it directs that all your remaining property be poured over into your living trust. That property must still go through probate on the way to your trust, however.

D. Do You Really Need a Living Trust?

Although a living trust is undoubtedly the most flexible way to avoid probate, not everyone needs one. Other, simpler probate-avoidance methods may better suit your stage of life. Here are a few factors to consider before you make your decision.

1. Your Age and Health

If you're young and healthy, your main estate planning goals are probably simple. You want to make sure that in the unlikely event of your early death, your property will go to the people or institutions you want to get it and, if you have young children, that they are well cared for. You don't need a trust to accomplish those ends. Writing a will (in which you name a guardian to raise the children), and perhaps buying some life insurance, would be easier, because a will is simpler to create than a living trust. Later in life, when you're in your 50s or 60s, you can set up a trust.

2. Your Home Life

Yes, it's true—the nature of your close relationships should have a big effect on your estate planning.

If you're married or are in a long-term relationship, you probably own many, if not all, of your valuable assets together with your mate. If you hold title in joint tenancy, tenancy by the entirety, or (in some states) community property, the property won't have to go through probate when the first owner dies. You may decide to wait to create a trust, which will avoid probate at the second death, until later. (Chapter 6 discusses joint ownership options.)

If you own property by yourself, though, you might want to take a closer look at setting up a living trust.

3. How Much You Own

Most states allow certain amounts or types of property to be transferred without probate, or by a streamlined court procedure, even if it's left by will. (See Chapter 8 for each state's rules.) If your estate is eligible for these simpler procedures, you may not need to go to the trouble of making and maintaining a trust.

And keep in mind that the more you own, the more your estate will owe for probate costs. It may not make sense to create a living trust until you've accumulated more assets.

4. What Kind of Assets You Own

Although a living trust can handle almost any kind of property, it's better suited to some types than others. (Section F, below, discusses in detail what to put into a trust and what to leave out.)

If your wealth is mostly in the form of real estate, a living trust may be a wise strategy for you. But if your money is in bank, brokerage, or retirement accounts, there are simpler and equally effective methods—for example, naming payable-on-death beneficiaries for each account. These methods don't offer all the features of a living trust—most important, you probably won't be able to name an alternate beneficiary. But especially for younger people, that drawback may be outweighed by ease and convenience. (Chapters 1 through 4 discuss these other methods.)

5. How Much You Owe

If you have a business that has many creditors, you may want your assets to go through probate, to take advantage of the cutoff period for creditors' claims that probate provides. If creditors don't make their claims by the deadline (in most states, a few months after probate proceedings are begun), they're out of luck. Your inheritors can take your property free of concern that creditors will surface later and attempt to claim a share.

E. Creating a Valid Living Trust

Setting up a valid living trust isn't difficult or expensive, but it does require a fair amount of paperwork—more, say, than just making a will does.

A MINI-GLOSSARY OF LIVING TRUST TERMS

You can't escape legal lingo entirely when you deal with living trusts. Keeping it to a minimum, here's what you need to know:

Someone who sets up a living trust is called a **grantor**, **trustor**, or **settlor**.

The property you transfer to the trust is called, collectively, the **trust property**, **trust principal**, or **trust estate**. (And, of course, there's a Latin version: the trust *corpus*.)

The person who has power over the trust property is called the **trustee**. In most instances, the person who sets up the trust (the grantor) is the original trustee of a living trust. If a married couple creates one shared marital trust, both are trustees.

The person the grantor names to take over as trustee after the grantor's death (or, with a shared marital trust, after the death of both spouses) is called the **successor trustee**. The successor trustee's job is to transfer the trust property to the beneficiaries, following the instructions in the Declaration of Trust. The successor trustee may also manage trust property inherited by young beneficiaries.

The people or organizations who inherit the trust property when the grantor dies are called **beneficiaries** of the trust.

---

1. Writing the Trust Document

The first step is to create a trust document. Lawyers commonly charge upwards of $1,000 to prepare a living trust, but you can do it yourself if you educate yourself with a good self-help book or software. (Nolo's living trust products are listed below.)

A trust document, formally known as a Declaration of Trust or trust instrument, is broadly similar to a will. It lists whom you want to inherit items of property. One way in which it differs from a will, however, is that it contains a list of property (usually called a schedule) that the trust owns. Another difference is that you can make a trust with your spouse; wills are normally for only one person.

A trust document should be signed in front of a notary public. You don't need to file it with any court or government office; just keep it in a safe place where the successor trustee will be able to get to it after your death.

 Doing it yourself. Nolo publishes both books and software that can help you learn about and prepare your own living trust.

Make Your Own Living Trust, by Denis Clifford. This book explains, step by step, how to create your own living trust. It contains instructions and forms for both a simple probate-avoidance trust and for an estate tax–saving (AB) trust, and explains how to decide which one you need.

Quicken WillMaker Plus software. You can make a probate-avoidance living trust, either for yourself or together with your spouse, with this easy-to-use software. You can also make a tax-saving AB trust. The legal manual that comes with the program discusses living trusts in depth.

Plan Your Estate, by Denis Clifford and Cora Jordan. This estate planning reference book offers information and advice on all kinds of estate planning strategies, including lots of material on wills and different kinds of probate-avoidance and tax-saving trusts.

2. Choosing a Successor Trustee

In your trust document, you must name someone to distribute your trust property to your beneficiaries after your death and to manage it before then if you become incapacitated. The legal term for this person is your successor trustee. (This jargon may be easier to remember if you keep in mind that you're the original trustee—this person is your successor.) To avoid conflicts, it's a good idea to name the same person to be both successor trustee and executor of your will.

Many people choose a grown son or daughter, other relative, or close friend to serve as successor trustee. It's perfectly legal to name a trust beneficiary—that is, someone who will receive trust property after your death. In fact, it's common.

Example: *Mildred names her only child, Allison, as both sole beneficiary of her living trust and successor trustee of the living trust. When Mildred dies, Allison uses her authority as trustee to transfer the trust property to herself.*

You should choose someone with good judgment, whose integrity you trust completely—and who is likely to outlive you. If you can't come up with anyone who fits this description, think twice about establishing a living trust.

Most people, however, won't have trouble picking a dependable, honest person. Great financial expertise is not usually necessary, because the successor trustee's job is to distribute your assets, not to manage property or investments over the long term (unless you become incapacitated and the trustee takes over before your death). A successor trustee who needs help from an accountant, lawyer, or tax preparer usually has authority, under the terms of the trust document, to pay for that help out of trust assets.

In most cases, it makes sense to name just one person as successor trustee, to avoid any possibility of conflicts that could hold up the distribution of trust property to your beneficiaries. But it's legal and may even be desirable to name more than one person. For example, you might name two or more of your children, if you don't expect any disagreements between them and fear that leaving one out would cause hurt feelings. You can also name an alternate successor trustee, in case your first choice isn't available when needed.

The successor trustee does not have to live in the same state as you do, though someone close by will probably have an easier job, especially with real estate transfers. But for transfers of property such as securities and bank accounts, it usually won't make much difference where the successor trustee lives.

INSTITUTIONS AS SUCCESSOR TRUSTEES

Your first choice as successor trustee should be a flesh-and-blood person, not the trust department of a bank or other institution. Institutional trustees charge hefty fees, which come out of the trust property and thus leave less for your family and friends. And most aren't interested in "small" trusts—ones that contain less than several hundred thousand dollars worth of property.

But if there's no close relative or friend you can appoint, consider naming a private trust company as successor trustee or as co-trustee with a person. As a rule they charge less than a bank, and your affairs will probably receive more personal attention.

Don't forget to ask. Before you finalize your living trust, check with the person you've chosen to be your successor trustee, and make sure your choice understands his or her responsibilities and is willing to serve.

Typically, the successor trustee of a simple probate-avoidance living trust isn't paid. This is because in most cases, the successor trustee's only job is to distribute the trust property to beneficiaries soon after the grantor's death. Often, the successor trustee inherits most of the trust property anyway.

An exception is a successor trustee who manages property that stays in trust for a child. In that case, the trust document commonly entitles the successor trustee to "reasonable compensation." The successor trustee decides what is reasonable and takes it from the trust property left to the young beneficiary.

3. Leaving Trust Property to Young Beneficiaries

If any of your beneficiaries might inherit trust property before they're legally adults (18, in most states), you should definitely arrange for an adult to manage the property on their behalf. Minors are not allowed to control significant amounts of property, and if you haven't provided someone to do it, a court may have to appoint a property guardian. You can, if you wish, also arrange for management for older beneficiaries who are adults in the eyes of the law, but not necessarily in yours.

There are two main ways to accomplish this goal:

- Leave the property in trust, to be managed by the successor trustee, or
- Name a custodian to manage the property.

Leaving the property in trust. In the trust document, you can state that if a beneficiary is under a certain age at your death, the property he or she is to inherit stays in trust. To distinguish it, the child's trust is often called a "subtrust" of the original living trust. The successor trustee (or your spouse, if you created a shared trust) manages the property until the beneficiary reaches the age you designated.

Example: *Roger leaves living trust property to his grandson, Alex, with the stipulation that if Alex is not yet 25 when Roger dies, the property will stay in trust to be used for his benefit. At Roger's death, Alex is just 17. The successor trustee of Roger's trust is his daughter Julia, who is Alex's mother. She takes control of the property, spending money on Alex's education and other allowed expenses, until his 25th birthday. Then he gets whatever is left.*

Naming a custodian. Instead of keeping the child's property in a trust, you may want instead to appoint a "custodian" to manage it. This option is available in all but a few states, under a law called the Uniform Transfers to Minors Act. (It's discussed fully in Chapter 1, Section C.)

The custodian you choose manages the property until the child reaches an age specified by your state's law: 21 in most states, but up to 25 in a few. Like a trustee, the custodian has a legal duty to act honestly and responsibly—but is not supervised by any court.

Dealing with banks and other institutions may also be easier for the custodian than for a trustee, because banks are familiar with the custodian's legal authority, which is determined by state law. A trustee's powers, on the other hand, come only from the trust document. Because every trust document is unique, a bank may want to examine yours and submit it for a review by bank lawyers, to make sure of the trustee's authority.

Because a custodianship must end at the age your state law dictates, it's not as flexible as a trust. But it works just fine if you don't leave a huge amount to the child and suspect that most of it will be spent by the time the child turns 21.

SAMPLE LIVING TRUST DOCUMENT (first page)

Declaration of Trust

Part 1. Trust Name
This revocable living trust shall be known as The Judith M. Avery Revocable Living Trust.

Part 2. Declaration of Trust
Judith M. Avery, called the grantor, declares that she has transferred and delivered to the trustee all her interest in the property described in Schedule A attached to this Declaration of Trust. All of that property is called the "trust property." The trustee hereby acknowledges receipt of the trust property and agrees to hold the trust property in trust, according to this Declaration of Trust.

The grantor may add property to the trust.

Part 3. Terminology
The term "this Declaration of Trust" includes any provisions added by valid amendment.

Part 4. Amendment and Revocation

A. Amendment or Revocation by Grantor
The grantor may amend or revoke this trust at any time, without notifying any beneficiary. An amendment must be made in writing and signed by the grantor. Revocation may be in writing or any manner allowed by law.

B. Amendment or Revocation by Other Person
The power to revoke or amend this trust is personal to the grantor. A conservator, guardian or other person shall not exercise it on behalf of the grantor, unless the grantor specifically grants a power to revoke or amend this trust in a Durable Power of Attorney.

Part 5. Payments From Trust During Grantor's Lifetime
The trustee shall pay to or use for the benefit of the grantor as much of the net income and principal of the trust property as the grantor requests. Income shall be paid to the grantor at least annually.

Part 6. Trustees

A. Trustee
Judith M. Avery shall be trustee of this trust.

B. Trustee's Responsibility
The trustee in office shall serve as trustee of all trusts created under this Declaration of Trust, including children's subtrusts.

4. Transferring Property to the Trust

Once you have a signed, notarized trust document, there is one more essential step to making your living trust effective. You must make sure that ownership of all the property you listed in the trust document is legally transferred to yourself as trustee of the living trust.

When living trusts fail, it is usually because the property listed in the trust document was not actually transferred to the trust. If property isn't properly transferred, the terms of the Declaration of Trust have no effect on it. At your death, it will pass under the terms of your will. If there is no will, it will go to your closest relatives under your state's "intestate succession" law.

Items with title documents. To transfer real estate, stocks, mutual funds, bonds, money market accounts, vehicles, or other property with title documents, you must change the title document to show that you own the property in your capacity as trustee. For example, if you want to put your house into your living trust, you must prepare and sign a new deed, transferring ownership from you to yourself as trustee.

Items without title documents. If an item of property doesn't have a title (ownership) document, listing it in the trust document is generally enough to transfer it. So, for example, no additional paperwork is required for most books, furniture, electronics, jewelry, appliances, musical instruments, and many other kinds of property. If, however, an item is particularly valuable, you may want to prepare a simple document that states you are officially transferring ownership to yourself as trustee. And if you're making a trust in New York, state law requires you to prepare a separate transfer document for all property.

F. What Property to Put in a Trust

You're creating a revocable living trust primarily to avoid probate fees. So here's the key rule to keep in mind: Generally, the more an item is worth, the more it will cost to probate it. That means if you create a trust, you should transfer at least your most valuable property items to it. Think about including:

- houses and other real estate
- stock, bond, and other security accounts held by brokerages (If you can't or don't want to name a T.O.D. beneficiary, see Chapter 3.)
- small business interests (stock in a closely held corporation, partnership interests, or limited liability company shares)
- patents and copyrights
- precious metals
- jewelry, antiques, furs, and valuable furniture
- valuable works of art, and
- valuable collections of stamps, coins, or other objects.

ADDING PROPERTY LATER

You can add property to your living trust at any time. And as trustee, you can always sell or give away property in the trust. You can also take it out of the living trust and put it back in your name as an individual.

You don't need to put everything you own into a living trust to save money on probate. For some assets, you may decide to use other probate-avoidance devices instead. (Some options are flagged below; also check the table in the Introduction for a thorough list of alternatives for different kinds of property.)

Even if some non-trust property does have to go through regular probate, attorney and appraisal fees generally correspond roughly to the value of the probated property, so they'll be relatively low.

1. Real Estate

If you're like most people, the most valuable thing you own is real estate: your house, condominium, or land. Many people create a living trust just to make sure a house doesn't go through probate. You can probably save your family substantial probate costs by transferring your real estate through a living trust.

Co-op apartments. If you own shares in a co-op corporation and want to transfer them to your living trust, you may run into difficulties with the corporation. Some (although this is fast changing) are reluctant to let a trustee—even though the trust is completely controlled by the grantor—own shares. Check the co-op corporation's rules to see if the transfer is allowed.

Look out for transfer taxes. In most states, transfers of real estate to revocable living trusts are exempt from transfer taxes usually imposed on real estate sales. But check with local property tax officials to make sure that transferring real estate to your living trust won't trigger a tax.

Check with the title company before you change title. A title company could take the position that holding real estate in trust cancels your title insurance policy. If this is a concern, check first.

Don't overlook simpler alternatives. If you already co-own real estate with someone else, you may not need a living trust right now. (See Chapter 5.) And in some states, you can prepare a deed now but have it take effect only at your death. These special "transfer-on-death" deeds are allowed in Arizona, Arkansas, Colorado, Kansas, Missouri, Nevada, New Mexico, and Ohio. They are discussed in Chapter 5.

2. Small Business Interests

Tying up an ongoing small business during probate can be disastrous. Not only does your executor have to run the business for many months, but a court must supervise. Using a living trust to transfer business interests to beneficiaries quickly after your death is almost essential if you want them to take over the business and keep it running.

Different kinds of business organizations present different issues when you want to transfer your interest to your living trust:

Sole proprietorships. If you (or you and your spouse) operate your business as a sole proprietorship, with all business assets held in your own name, you can simply transfer your business property to your living trust as you would any other property. You should also transfer the business's name itself: that transfers the customer goodwill associated with the name.

Partnership interests. If you operate your business with partners, you should be able to easily transfer your partnership share to your living trust. If there is a partnership ownership certificate, it must be changed to include the trust as owner of your share.

Some partnership agreements require that a deceased partner's share of the business must be offered to the other partners; only if they decline to buy it for a fair price does it go to the inheritors. But that happens after death, so it shouldn't affect your ability to transfer the property to your living trust now.

It's not common, but a partnership agreement may limit or forbid transfers to a living trust. If yours does, you and your partners may want to see a lawyer before you make any changes.

Closely held corporations. A closely held corporation is a corporation that is not authorized to sell shares to the public. All its shares are owned by a few people (or just one) who are actively involved in running the business (or are relatives of people who are). Normally, you can use a living trust to transfer shares in a closely held corporation by listing the stock in the trust document and then having the stock certificates reissued in your name as trustee.

You'll want to check the corporation's bylaws and any shareholders' agreements, in case there are restrictions on your freedom to transfer your shares to a living trust. Also make sure that if you hold the shares in trust, you will still have voting rights in your capacity as trustee of the living trust; usually, this is not a problem. If it is, you and the other shareholders should be able to amend the corporation's bylaws to allow it.

One fairly common rule is that surviving shareholders (or the corporation itself) have the right to buy the shares of a deceased shareholder. In that case, you can still use a living trust to transfer the shares, but the people who inherit them may have to sell them to the other shareholders.

Limited liability companies. If your small business is an LLC, you'll need the consent of a majority or all of the other owners (check your operating agreement) before you can transfer your interest to your living trust. Getting the other owners to agree shouldn't be a problem; they'll just want to know that you, as trustee of your own trust, will have authority to vote on LLC decisions. You may also want to modify your trust document to give the trustee (that's you) specific authority to participate in the limited liability company. Another way to address this concern would be to transfer your economic interest in the LLC, but not your right to vote. The transfer itself isn't hard—you can prepare your own form and call it an Assignment of Interest.

3. Bank Accounts

It's not difficult to hold bank accounts in your living trust. You just need to change the paperwork held by the bank, savings and loan, or credit union.

It's sometimes inconvenient, however, to have bank accounts owned in the name of a trust. That's especially true for personal checking accounts—it's not always easy to write a check at a convenience store at 10 p.m. if the account is owned by a revocable living trust.

Consider the alternatives. Instead of using a living trust, consider adding a payable-on-death beneficiary to your account. At your death, what's left in those accounts will go directly to the beneficiary, without probate. (See Chapter 1.)

4. Individual Retirement Accounts

Individual retirement accounts can't be assigned to a trust; you, as an individual, must own your accounts. You can, however, name a trust as a beneficiary. (See Chapter 2.)

5. Vehicles

Some kinds of property are cumbersome to keep in a living trust. It's not a legal problem, just a practical one. Cars or other vehicles you use regularly are a good example. Having registration and insurance in the trustee's name could be confusing, and some lenders and insurance companies are flummoxed by cars that technically are owned by living trusts.

If you have valuable antique autos, or a mobile home that is permanently attached to land and considered real estate under your state's law, however, you may want to go ahead and transfer ownership to your living trust. You should be able to find an insurance company that will cooperate.

💡 **Check out special transfer procedures for vehicles.** Chapter 4 discusses several ways, simpler than a living trust, to avoid probate for vehicles.

6. Property You Buy or Sell Frequently

If you don't expect to own an item of property at your death, there's no compelling reason to transfer it to your living trust. Remember, the probate process you want to avoid doesn't happen until after your death. On the other hand, if you're buying property, it's usually not much more trouble to acquire and own it in the name of the trust.

Stocks and bonds. Even if you buy and sell securities regularly, there's no problem with having them in a living trust. See Section 8, below.

7. Life Insurance

If you own a life insurance policy at your death, the proceeds that the named beneficiary receives do not go through probate. (They are, however, considered part of your estate for federal estate tax purposes.)

If a child is the beneficiary of your policy, however, you may want to take an additional step to make sure someone will manage the money for the child if necessary. It's not difficult; you just name your living trust as the beneficiary. Then, in the trust document, specify that the proceeds should be managed by an adult if the child is still young when you die. If you don't arrange for management of the money, and the child receives the money while still a minor, a court will have to appoint a financial guardian to handle the money.

8. Securities

It's easy to register stocks, bonds, and mutual funds as trustee of your living trust; all brokers and mutual fund companies will help you. It's even easier if you set up accounts to consolidate all your investments at a big investment company such as Charles Schwab, Vanguard, or Fidelity. You can put your whole account into the living trust, and then automatically buy and sell securities in the name of the trustee.

Once the account is in the trustee's name, all securities in the account are then held in trust. That means you can use your living trust to leave all the contents of the account to a specific beneficiary. If you want to leave stock to different beneficiaries, you can either establish more than one brokerage account or leave the contents of a single account to more than one beneficiary to own together.

Stock in closely held corporations. See Section 2, Small Business Interests, above.

Consider transfer-on-death registration instead. Almost all states now allow ownership of securities to be registered in "transfer-on-death" form. In those states, you can designate someone to receive your securities, including mutual funds and brokerage accounts, after your death. No probate will be necessary. (See Chapter 3.)

9. Cash

It's common for people to want to leave cash to beneficiaries—for example, to leave $5,000 to a relative, friend, or charity. There's no way, however, to transfer cash to a living trust.

You can, however, easily accomplish the same goal by transferring ownership of a cash account—savings account, money market account, or certificate of deposit, for example—to your living trust. You can then name a beneficiary to receive the contents of the account. So if you want to leave $5,000 to cousin Fred, all you have to do is put the money in a bank or money market account, transfer it to yourself as trustee and name Fred, in the trust document, as the beneficiary.

If you don't want to set up a separate account to leave a modest amount of cash to a beneficiary, think about buying a savings bond and designating a payable-on-death beneficiary, or leaving one larger account, through your trust, to several beneficiaries.

G. Taxes and Recordkeeping

After a revocable living trust is created, little day-to-day recordkeeping is required.

Whenever you transfer property to or from the trust, however, it must be done in writing. That isn't difficult unless you transfer a lot of property in and out of the trust.

Example: *Monica and David Fielding put their house in a living trust to avoid probate, but later decide to sell it. In the real estate contract and deed transferring ownership to the new owners, Monica and David sign their names "as trustees of the Monica and David Fielding Revocable Living Trust."*

REGISTERING THE TRUST

Some states (Alaska, Colorado, Florida, Hawaii, Idaho, Maine, Michigan, Missouri, Nebraska, and North Dakota) require that you register your living trust document with the local court. But there are no legal consequences or penalties if you don't. Registration entails filing some basic information about the trust—not all its terms—with the court.

No separate income tax records or returns are necessary as long as you are both the grantor and the trustee. (IRS Reg. § 1.671-4.) Income from property in the living trust must be reported on your personal income tax return; you don't have to file a separate tax return for the trust.

H. Amending or Revoking a Living Trust Document

One of the most attractive features of a revocable living trust is its flexibility: You can change its terms, or end it altogether, at any time.

If you created a shared trust with your spouse, either of you can revoke it. If, however, you want to change any trust provisions—for example, change a beneficiary or successor trustee—both of you must agree in writing. And both spouses will probably have to consent to transfer real estate out of the living trust; buyers and title insurance companies usually insist on both spouses' signatures on transfer documents. After one spouse dies, the surviving spouse is free to amend the terms of the trust document that deal with his or her property, but can't change the parts that determine what happens to the deceased spouse's trust property.

Even if you want to make substantial changes, you will probably want to amend your living trust document, not revoke it. It might, at first glance, seem easier to revoke the document and start again, as you might with a will. But if you revoke your living trust and create another one, you must transfer all the trust property out of the old living trust and into the new one.

AMENDING OR REVOKING YOUR LIVING TRUST

You may need to amend if...	You may need to revoke if...
You get married.	You want to make extensive, possibly confusing revisions.
You have a child.	You get divorced.
You add valuable property to the trust.	
You change your mind about whom you want to inherit certain items of trust property or whom you want to serve as successor trustee.	
You move to a state with different laws about marital property or property management for young beneficiaries.	
Your spouse dies.	
A major beneficiary dies.	

CHAPTER 8

Take Advantage of Special Procedures for Small Estates

Probate has a deservedly bad name, and the best solution would be to do away with it for uncontested cases—but that's too radical for lawyer-dominated legislatures. So in a half-hearted but still helpful response, states have begun to let some people slip out of the probate requirement.

Who gets out? As you might guess, one big category comprises people who don't leave much of monetary value—and whose probate cases therefore aren't worth much to lawyers. "Small estates are a plague to the courts and lawyers as well as the debtors," wrote one official commentator dismissively. (Comments to Ind. Stat. Ann. § 29-1-8-1.)

Because of the way the laws are written, however, not only small estates can benefit. Many large estates—worth hundreds of thousands of dollars—legally qualify as "small estates," eligible for special transfer procedures that speed property to inheritors.

There are two basic kinds of probate shortcuts for small estates:

- **Claiming property with affidavits—no court required.** If the total value of all the assets you leave behind is less than a certain amount, the people who inherit your personal property—that's anything except real estate—may be able to skip probate entirely. The exact amount depends on state law, and varies hugely. Wyoming's limit, $150,000, is the highest.

  If the estate qualifies, an inheritor can prepare a short document stating that he or she is entitled to a certain item of property under a will or state law. This paper, signed under oath, is called an affidavit. When the person or institution holding the prop-erty—for example, a bank where the deceased person had an account—receives the affidavit and a copy of the death certificate, it releases the money or other property.

- **Simplified court procedures.** Another option for small estates (again, as defined by state law) is a quicker, simpler version of probate. The probate court is still involved, but it exerts far less control over the settling of the estate. In many states, these procedures are straightforward enough to handle without a lawyer, so they save money as well as time.

Most states have both kinds of procedures; some have just one. A complete state-by-state listing appears later in the chapter.

A. Why Even Large Estates May Qualify

If you're sure that you will leave behind assets worth much more than your state's dollar limit, you probably assume that the simple procedures described in this chapter won't be available to your inheritors. Not so fast. Even if the value of your estate is bigger—much bigger—than your state's limit, your inheritors may still be able to take advantage of the simpler procedures.

The reason is that in adding up the value of your estate to see if it is under the dollar limit, many states exclude huge chunks of assets. It's conceivable that in some states, a $500,000 estate could qualify for "small estate" procedures.

If you plan ahead and learn about your state's rules (keeping in mind, of course, that they may change before your death), chances are good that you can adjust your affairs so that you will leave a "small estate" as your state defines it.

You can find summaries of each state's rules later in this chapter. The rest of this section tells you what to look for and how to make sense of what you find.

1. What Kinds of Property Count

Many states simply don't consider the value of certain kinds of valuable property—for example, motor vehicles, real estate, or real estate located in another state. And possibly more important, many states don't count the value of property that won't go through probate. That means your probate-avoidance work pays double dividends after your death. Making sure your bank accounts and real estate won't go through probate, for example, not only saves on those probate costs but might also enable other property to escape probate, too.

Example 1: *Robert, a California resident, dies owning a car worth $18,000 and a half-interest in these assets, worth almost $300,000:*

- *an IRA worth $50,000*

- *a payable-on-death bank account with $10,000 in it*

- *$20,000 worth of stocks, and*

- *a house worth $400,000, which he owns as community property with right of survivorship with his wife.*

The limit for "small estates" in California is only $100,000, but vehicles, payable-on-death accounts, and property that goes to a surviving spouse aren't counted toward that limit. So only the stocks count toward the $100,000 limit, allowing Robert's estate to qualify for small estate procedures.

Example 2: *Tina lives in Indiana, which restricts use of its affidavit procedure to estates worth no more than $25,000. That won't help me, thinks Tina, who expects to leave about $200,000 worth of property at her death. But she's wrong. When it comes to this limit, Indiana, like a fair number of other states, only counts assets that would otherwise go through probate.*

Here's how Tina's $200,000 estate breaks down:

- *her house, worth $80,000, which she has transferred to a living trust to avoid probate*

- *securities, worth $40,000, that she has registered in beneficiary form*

- *payable-on-death bank accounts containing $30,000*
- *a $40,000 retirement account for which she's named a beneficiary, and*
- *miscellaneous personal property and household items worth $10,000.*

Because only the $10,000 of miscellaneous items are subject to probate, Tina has a "small estate" under Indiana law. Her inheritors will be able to use the affidavit procedure to claim the household items, and no probate will be necessary.

2. Subtracting What You Owe on Property

When you're trying to figure out whether or not your estate will be small enough to escape probate, some states require you to use the market value of your property; others instruct you to subtract any amounts owed on it. It can make a huge difference, of course.

Example: *Millie, a childless widow, dies owning personal property—a car, some stocks, bank accounts, and household furnishings—with a total market value of $55,000. Arizona law says that her inheritors can claim the property without probate if the total value, less "liens and encumbrances," is no greater than $50,000. Because Millie still owed $7,000 on her car when she died, that amount (a lien on the car) can be subtracted. That brings the total value of her estate to $48,000—low enough to qualify for the small estate procedure.*

3. If There's No Dollar Limit

When it comes to determining who can use simplified probate, a fair number of states don't specify a dollar amount as an upper limit. Instead, they grant small estate status to estates that will be used up by paying certain high-priority debts: the family allowance mandated by law, reasonable funeral and burial expenses, and medical costs of the last illness. The reasoning is that if there's nothing left for other creditors, there's no need for a probate court proceeding. Obviously, estates of very different size will qualify, depending on the debts of the deceased person.

4. Using These Rules to Plan

Your state's definition of a small estate is the final piece in the entire probate-avoidance puzzle. Once you understand it, you'll know how much effort you need to devote to other probate-avoidance methods.

For example, say you discover that your state allows up to $70,000 to be transferred by affidavit, and only property that is subject to probate counts toward that limit. You'll know that as long as your most valuable items avoid probate, your executor will be able to use the small estate procedures for a big pile of miscellaneous assets that you have left through your will.

Educate your executor. Even if your estate qualifies for a simplified probate procedure, it won't do you any good unless your executor knows that the option is available. Too many confused or intimidated executors simply turn everything over to a lawyer, and pay the price.

B. Claiming Wages With an Affidavit

Most states allow a surviving spouse or other family member to immediately collect, without involving the probate court, salary or wages that were earned by the deceased person. There may be a cap of a few hundred or thousand dollars on the amount that can be collected this way.

Commonly, all the family member needs to do is submit a short statement, signed in front of a notary public, to the employer. It's even simpler than preparing an affidavit under the general procedure, and there's no waiting period. A sample affidavit is shown below.

Most large employers are familiar with this kind of form; smaller ones, which might have paid the surviving spouse the money even without a formal request, will probably be reassured by it.

SAMPLE AFFIDAVIT FOR COLLECTING WAGES

Affidavit for Collection of Compensation Owed Deceased Spouse

I, the undersigned, state as follows:

1. Harold T. Ericson, the decedent, died on July 16, 20xx, at Charleston, West Virginia.

2. I am the surviving spouse of the decedent.

3. No proceeding for the administration of the decedent's estate is pending or has been conducted in any jurisdiction.

4. West Virginia Code § 21-5-8a requires that earnings of the decedent, including compensation for unused vacation, up to $800, be paid promptly to the surviving spouse.

5. I request that I be paid any compensation owed by you for personal services of the decedent, including compensation for unused vacation, not to exceed $800.

6. I declare under penalty of perjury of the laws of West Virginia that the foregoing is true and correct.

_____   _____
Sarah M. Ericson   Date
.......[notarization]

C. Claiming Other Property With Affidavits

An affidavit procedure, happily, dispenses with probate court altogether. If everything in your estate qualifies for this procedure, a probate court will never need to get involved after your death. Instead, inheritors prepare and sign a brief affidavit (sworn statement) saying that they are entitled to use the procedure and to inherit a particular item of property. (There's a sample affidavit, so you can see what one looks like, later in this section.) Then, to get actual possession of the asset, they simply present the affidavit to the person or institution, such as a bank or broker, holding the asset.

There are severe restrictions, however, on who can use this method:

- The property left by the deceased person must be worth less than the ceiling set by state law. These limits vary widely. (Some kinds of property, however, may not count toward the limit, as discussed in Section A, above.)

- In most states, the procedure can't be used to transfer real estate. A handful of states, however, do provide a special affidavit procedure for real estate. But because real estate transfers are always a matter of public record, the affidavit must be filed in court or with a public agency.

- In most states, inheritors cannot use the affidavit procedure if regular probate court proceedings have begun.

Inheritors can use an affidavit to collect their property whether or not there was a will. In the affidavit, they usually state whether they are inheriting under the terms of a will or under state law. If there's no valid will, your state's "intestate succession" law determines who inherits property. The intestate succession formula is slightly different from state to state, but generally if there are a surviving spouse and children, they inherit everything. If not, then parents, grandchildren, or siblings are next in line.

AFFIDAVIT PROCEDURE AT A GLANCE

Pros

- Doesn't require any action on your part except making sure your executor knows the procedure may be available.

- Simple for your executor to do, and costs nothing.

Cons

- Dollar limits restrict procedure to small estates, as that's defined by your state's law.

- Can't be used for real estate, except in a few states.

- There is a waiting period after death; property can't be transferred to beneficiaries for a month or two.

- Not available in all states.

1. Claiming the Property

The process of transferring your property to its new owners will be initiated by the people who are inheriting it. Usually, there is a short waiting period—commonly, 30 or 45 days after the death—before anyone is allowed to collect the property.

To get the property, they will present their affidavits and a copy of the death certificate to the person or institution who has possession of the property. Some institutions may also insist on seeing a copy of the will, if any. If the affidavit appears truthful, that person or institution is allowed, by law, to turn over the property without investigating the truth of the statements in the affidavit.

Example: *In his will, Perry leaves $20,000 to Alice. A month after Perry dies, Alice goes to his bank and fills out the affidavit form she picks up there, swearing that she is entitled to the money and that the estate qualifies for the state's small estate affidavit procedure. The bank, after looking at the affidavit, a copy of Perry's death certificate and possibly the will, transfers $20,000 from Perry's account to her.*

Banks, other financial institutions, and state motor vehicles agencies, which deal with this sort of transfer all the time, may have their own affidavit forms for people to fill out. Otherwise, the claimants may have to put together their own, making sure it covers all the conditions the state statute requires. Generally, an affidavit must include statements to the effect that:

- The value of the probate estate does not exceed the statutory limit.
- The required waiting period has elapsed since the death.
- No probate court proceedings have been initiated.
- The claimant is entitled to the property. Although it's not always required by statute, it's a good idea for the claimant to explain the basis of the claim—for example, because of the deceased person's will or state intestate succession law.

The affidavit may need to be notarized—that is, signed in front of a notary public—or it may be enough for it to include a statement to the effect that it is being signed "under penalty of perjury."

A sample affidavit, from Minnesota, is shown below.

SAMPLE AFFIDAVIT

Affidavit for Collection of Personal Property Under Minnesota Statutes 524.3-1201

I, the undersigned, state as follows:

1. _____, the decedent, died on _____.

2. The value of the entire probate estate, determined as of the date of death, wherever located, including specifically any contents of a safe deposit box, less liens and encumbrances, does not exceed $20,000.

3. At least thirty days have elapsed since the decedent's death, as shown by the attached certified copy of the decedent's death certificate.

4. No application or petition for the appointment of a personal representative is pending or has been granted in any jurisdiction.

5. I, the undersigned, am entitled to payment or delivery, under the terms of the decedent's will, of the following property:

_____

_____

_____

6. I declare that the foregoing is true and correct.

_____   _____

Signature   Date

.......[notarization]

In most states, an affidavit needs to be given only to the entity that is holding the property. But some states now require a copy to be sent to the state taxing agency, in case any state taxes are due. If the decedent received any public benefits, another copy may need to go to the Health or Welfare Department; if there's money left in the estate, the government will want to be reimbursed for the aid it provided.

Most banks, brokers, and other entities your inheritors will likely deal with are quite familiar with the affidavit process. But if one refuses to cooperate, just showing an unhelpful clerk a copy of the statute (readily available online or at a public law library) should melt away the opposition. If that doesn't get results, chances are a phone call or letter from a local lawyer will. And as a last resort, the inheritor can go to court—small claims court, if possible—and demand that the assets be turned over.

Help for California readers. For a tear-out California affidavit form and instructions on how to use it, see *How to Probate an Estate in California,* by Julia Nissley (Nolo).

2. State Rules

Here are the rules for each state on when inheritors can use the affidavit procedure.

STATE	OUT-OF-COURT AFFIDAVIT PROCEDURE
Alabama	None
Alaska	For estates of up to $15,000, less liens and encumbrances. Can't be used to transfer real estate. *Alaska Stat. § 13.16.680*
Arizona	Available if value of all personal property in estate, less liens and encumbrances, is $50,000 or less. Can't be used for real estate. *Ariz. Rev. Stat. § 14-3971(B)*
Arkansas	None

STATE	OUT-OF-COURT AFFIDAVIT PROCEDURE (cont.)
California	1. For estates of up to $100,000.
	Excluded from calculating value of estate: real estate outside California; joint tenancy property; property that goes outright to a surviving spouse; life insurance, death benefits and other assets not subject to probate that pass to named beneficiaries; multiple-party accounts and payable-on-death accounts; any registered manufactured or mobile home; any numbered vessel; any registered motor vehicle; salary up to $5,000; amounts due decedent for services in the armed forces; property held in trust, including a living trust. *Cal. Prob. Code §§ 13050, 13100 and following*
	2. For real estate up to $20,000 in value. Inheritors can file fill-in-the-blanks affidavit with probate court and then record a certified copy with county recorder. *Cal. Prob. Code §§ 13200 to 13208*
Colorado	For estates where fair market value of property that is subject to disposition by will or state intestate succession law, less liens and encumbrances, does not exceed $50,000. (This excludes joint tenancy property, property in a living trust, payable-on-death bank accounts, and other kinds of property that don't pass under a will.) Can't be used to transfer real estate. *Colo. Rev. Stat. § 15-12-1201*
Connecticut	None
Delaware	For estates without solely owned Delaware real estate and a value of no more than $30,000. (Jointly owned property, and death benefits that pass outside of probate, such as insurance or pension proceeds, are not counted toward the $30,000 limit.) Available only to spouse, certain relatives, or funeral director. *Del. Code Ann. tit. 12, § 2306*
District of Columbia	Only if deceased person owned nothing but one or two motor vehicles. *D.C. Code Ann. § 20-357*

STATE	OUT-OF-COURT AFFIDAVIT PROCEDURE (cont.)
Florida	None
Georgia	None
Hawaii	Available if value of property (excluding any motor vehicles) deceased person owned in Hawaii doesn't exceed $100,000. Can't be used to transfer real estate. *Haw. Rev. Stat. §§ 560:3-1201 and following*
Idaho	Available if fair market value of estate subject to probate, wherever located, less liens and encumbrances, doesn't exceed $75,000. Can't be used to transfer real estate. *Idaho Code §§ 15-3-1201 and following*
Illinois	Available if gross value of all deceased person's property that passes under a will or by state law, excluding real estate, did not exceed $100,000. Can't be used to transfer real estate. Statute contains a fill-in-the-blanks affidavit. *755 Ill. Comp. Stat. § 5/25-1*
Indiana	Value of gross probate estate, less liens and encumbrances, must not exceed $25,000. Can't be used to transfer real estate. *Ind. Code Ann. § 29-1-8-1*
Iowa	Available if there is no real estate (or real estate passes to surviving spouse as joint tenant) and gross value of the deceased person's personal property doesn't exceed $25,000. *Iowa Code § 633.356*
Kansas	Available if total assets of the deceased person's estate do not exceed $20,000 in value. Can't be used to transfer real estate. The state judicial council provides a fill-in-the-blanks affidavit. *Kan. Stat. Ann. § 59-1507b*
Kentucky	None
Louisiana	This book doesn't cover Louisiana law.
Maine	Available if value of the entire estate, wherever located, less liens and encumbrances, does not exceed $10,000. Can't be used to transfer real estate. *Me. Rev. Stat. Ann. tit.18-A, §§ 3-1201 and following*

STATE	OUT-OF-COURT AFFIDAVIT PROCEDURE (cont.)
Maryland	None
Massachusetts	None
Michigan	Available if estate does not include real estate and value of the entire estate, less liens and encumbrances, doesn't exceed $15,000. The state courts will provide a standardized form for the affidavit. *Mich. Comp. Laws § 700.3983*
Minnesota	$20,000 limit for entire probate estate, wherever located, including any contents of a safe deposit box, less liens and encumbrances. Can't be used to transfer real estate. *Minn. Stat. § 524.3-1201*
Mississippi	None
Missouri	None
Montana	Available if value of entire estate, wherever located, less liens and encumbrances, is $50,000 or less. Can't be used to transfer real estate. *Mont. Code Ann. § 72-3-1101*
Nebraska	Available if value of the entire estate, wherever located, less liens and encumbrances, is $25,000 or less. Can't be used to transfer real estate. *Neb. Rev. Stat. § 30-24,125*
Nevada	Available if decedent owned no real estate in Nevada and gross value of property in Nevada doesn't exceed $20,000. Only surviving spouse, children, grandchildren, parents, or siblings can use the procedure. *Nev. Rev. Stat. Ann. § 146.080*
New Hampshire	None
New Jersey	None

STATE	OUT-OF-COURT AFFIDAVIT PROCEDURE (cont.)
New Mexico	1. For real estate: If married couple owns principal residence, valued for property tax purposes at $100,000 or less, as community property, surviving spouse may file affidavit with county clerk if no other assets require probate. *N.M. Stat. Ann. 45-3-1205* 2. For other property: Available if value of entire estate, wherever located, less liens and encumbrances, is $30,000 or less. *N.M. Stat. Ann. § 45-3-1201*
New York	None
North Carolina	Available if value of the personal property, less liens and encumbrances, is $10,000 or less ($20,000 if the surviving spouse is the sole heir). *N.C. Gen. Stat. §§ 28A-25-1 and following*
North Dakota	Available if value of entire estate subject to probate, less liens and encumbrances, is $50,000 or less. Can't be used to transfer real estate. *N.D. Cent. Code §§ 30.1-23-01 and following*
Ohio	None
Oklahoma	None
Oregon	None
Pennsylvania	None
Rhode Island	None
South Carolina	Available if value of property passing by will or under law, less liens and encumbrances, is $10,000 or less. Affidavit must be approved by probate judge. Can't be used to transfer real estate. *S.C. Code Ann. § 62-3-1201*
South Dakota	Available if value of entire estate, less liens and encumbrances, is $50,000 or less. Can't be used to transfer real estate. *S.D. Codified Laws §§ 29A-3-1201 and following*
Tennessee	None

STATE	OUT-OF-COURT AFFIDAVIT PROCEDURE (cont.)
Texas	Available if there is no will, and value of entire estate, not including homestead and exempt property, does not exceed $50,000. Probate judge must approve affidavit. Can be used to transfer homestead, but no other real estate. *Tex. Prob. Code Ann. § 137*
Utah	Available if value of entire estate subject to probate, less liens and encumbrances, is $25,000 or less. May also transfer up to four boats, motor vehicles, trailers, or semi-trailers if value of estate subject to probate, excluding the value of the vehicles, is $25,000 or less. Can't be used to transfer real estate. *Utah Code Ann. § 75-3-1201*
Vermont	None
Virginia	1. Available if entire personal probate estate does not exceed $15,000. Can't be used to transfer real estate. *Va. Code Ann. § 64.1-132.2* 2. Amounts of less than $15,000 that are owed the decedent for wages, union death benefits, state or federal benefits, or from a trust or estate; vessels registered with the U.S. Bureau of Customs; and securities worth less than $15,000 can be transferred to surviving spouse or inheritors without probate. *Va. Code Ann. §§ 64.1-123 and following*
Washington	Available if value of assets subject to probate, not counting surviving spouse's community property interest, less liens and encumbrances, is $60,000 or less. Can't be used to transfer real estate. *Wash. Rev. Code Ann. §§ 11.62.010 and following*
West Virginia	None
Wisconsin	Available if decedent's solely owned property in Wisconsin is worth $20,000 or less. *Wis. Stat. Ann. § 867.03*
Wyoming	Available if value of entire estate, less liens and encumbrances, is $150,000 or less. Can't be used to transfer real estate. Affidavit must be filed with county clerk. *Wyo. Stat. § 2-1-201*

D. Simplified Court Procedures

Even if your estate doesn't qualify for the affidavit procedure, or not all your property can be transferred that way, there may still be hope for avoiding a full-fledged probate proceeding. Nearly all states offer something called "summary probate" or "informal probate," which is more complex than the out-of-court affidavit procedure but not nearly as bothersome as regular probate.

SIMPLIFIED PROBATE AT A GLANCE

Pros	Cons
• Doesn't require any action on your part except making sure your executor knows the procedure may be available.	• Dollar limits restrict procedure to small estates, as that's defined by your state's law.
• A good fallback for property you don't specifically use a probate-avoidance method for.	• In some states, limited to surviving spouse or children.
	• There is a waiting period after death; property can't be transferred to beneficiaries for a month or two.
	• Your executor may need to hire a lawyer.
	• Not available in all states.

---

1. An Overview

A summary probate is started by the person named in the will to serve as executor (also called personal representative) of the estate. (If there's no will, the surviving spouse, or another relative who stands to inherit, usually takes the initiative.) That person—let's call him or her the executor, which is what most courts do—files a document (commonly called a petition or affidavit) with the local probate court, requesting the simpler process. Most states impose a waiting period of a month or two before the petition may be filed. Specific requirements vary from state to state, but in most cases the petition must:

- say that the estate qualifies as a "small estate," as state law defines that term
- list the persons or organizations entitled to inherit the property
- state that no request for formal probate has been made, and
- state that all (or certain) debts and taxes have been paid.

The executor will probably also need to submit a copy of the death certificate, the deceased person's will, if there is one, and an inventory and appraisal of all the deceased person's assets.

If everything is in order, the probate court will authorize the summary procedure, and basically that's the end of court supervision. The executor may be required to notify creditors and people who might inherit (under the will or state law) of the death and the probate proceedings, or to publish a notice in a local newspaper. Many states, however, don't require this. Otherwise, the bills can be paid and the assets distributed immediately, without further ado. Generally, the executor is also required to file a closing statement with the court, showing where everything went.

Use simplified probate as interim estate planning. Conducting a simplified probate procedure, while an improvement over regular probate, still isn't nearly as easy as winding up a living trust or using the other probate-avoidance methods in this book. For most people, it's best to think of simplified probate as a fallback method of avoiding probate; if you're young and healthy, you may decide to put off creating a trust until later in life, knowing that if necessary, simplified probate procedures will ease things for your loved ones.

2. Is a Lawyer Necessary?

Even a new-and-improved simple probate may still require a fair amount of paperwork. Everything can, however, probably be done by mail; no court appearances should be necessary.

How easy it will be for someone to tackle a summary probate depends to a large extent on whether or not you can find a good self-help book and on how helpful the probate court is. Some courts provide good explanatory materials and forms, and court clerks help people along. Others, unfortunately, expect people to figure out every detail themselves.

If that's the situation where you live, someone who goes this route after your death may want to get advice from an experienced lawyer or paralegal. That doesn't mean turning the whole process over to a professional—but having someone available to help smooth over any rough patches can make a huge difference.

Even if a lawyer is consulted, the overall cost of simplified probate should be less than that of regular probate. The process will be over more quickly, too.

Help for California readers. For complete instructions on handling a summary probate without a lawyer in California, see *How to Probate an Estate in California*, by Julia Nissley (Nolo).

3. State Rules

Brief descriptions of who qualifies for each state's simplified probate procedures are listed below.

Each state's actual court procedure, however, is different. If you're interested in the details—what kind of documents are currently required and how long the process takes—you'll have to ask someone at your local court or read your state's statutes themselves. You can find a statute online or at a large public library or county law library, by looking up its citation (listed after each description): If you're looking online, start at www.nolo.com and follow the links to your state's statutes. If you go to a library, a law librarian can quickly help you get to the right book. Keep in mind, though, that these statutes change; years from now, the rules and procedures may be very different.

STATE	SIMPLIFIED COURT PROCEDURE
Alabama	For estates with no real estate and a value of no more than $3,000. *Ala. Code §§ 43-2-690 and following*
Alaska	Available if value of the entire estate, less liens and encumbrances, does not exceed homestead allowance, exempt property, family allowance, costs and expenses of administration, funeral expenses, and medical and hospital expenses of the last illness. *Alaska Stat. §§ 13.16.690, 695*
Arizona	1. For real estate, if value of all property in estate, less liens and encumbrances on the real estate, does not exceed $50,000. Inheritors can file affidavit in court. *Ariz. Rev. Stat. Ann. §§ 14-3971(E), 14-3973* 2. Available if value of the entire estate, less liens and encumbrances, does not exceed allowance in lieu of homestead, exempt property, family allowance, costs of administration, funeral expenses, and medical and hospital expenses of the last illness. *Ariz. Rev. Stat. Ann. §§ 14-3973, 3974*
Arkansas	1. For estates where personal property does not exceed that to which the widow, if any, or minor children, if any, are by law entitled free of debt, as dower or curtesy and statutory allowances. Probate court can order entire estate to widow and/or minor children. *Ark. Code Ann. § 28-41-103*

STATE	SIMPLIFIED COURT PROCEDURE (cont.)
Arkansas (cont.)	2. For estates where the value, less encumbrances, of all property owned by the decedent, excluding the homestead of and the statutory allowances for the benefit of a spouse or minor children, if any, does not exceed $100,000. *Ark. Code Ann. § 28-41-101*
California	For estates up to $100,000 in value. (For how this amount is calculated, see California entry in Affidavit Procedure Table, Section C, above.) *Cal. Prob. Code §§ 13150 and following*
Colorado	For estates where the value of the entire estate, less liens and encumbrances, does not exceed the value of personal property held by the decedent as fiduciary or trustee, exempt property allowance, family allowance, costs of administration, funeral expenses, and medical expenses of the last illness. *Colo. Rev. Stat. § 15-12-1203*
Connecticut	For estates without real estate, not exceeding $20,000 in value. *Conn. Gen. Stat. § 45a-273*
Delaware	None
District of Columbia	For estates where property subject to administration in D.C. has value of $40,000 or less. *D.C. Code Ann. § 20-351 and following*
Florida	1. For estates where no real estate is left and all property is exempt from creditors' claims except amounts needed to pay funeral and two months' last illness expenses. Upon letter to court, court will authorize transfer of property to people entitled to it. *Fla. Stat. Ann. § 735.301*
	2. For estates where value of entire estate subject to administration in Florida, less the value of property that is exempt from creditors' claims, doesn't exceed $75,000, OR decedent has been dead more than two years. Petition must be filed with court. *Fla. Stat. Ann. §§ 735.201 and following*

STATE	SIMPLIFIED COURT PROCEDURE (cont.)
Georgia	Available if there is no will, estate owes no debts, and all heirs have amicably agreed on how to divide the property. *Ga. Code Ann. §§ 53-2-40 and following*
Hawaii	Available if value of all property deceased person owned in Hawaii doesn't exceed $100,000. Any interested person can request summary probate. Court handles distribution for fee of 3% of market value of first $100,000 of gross estate. *Haw. Rev. Stat. §§ 560:3-1205 and following*
Idaho	1. Available if value of all property deceased person owned, less liens and encumbrances, doesn't exceed the homestead allowance, exempt property, family allowance, costs of administration, funeral expenses, and medical expenses of the last illness. *Idaho Code §§ 15-3-1203 and following* 2. A surviving spouse who inherits everything can file petition with court, which will issue a decree to that effect. *Idaho Code § 15-3-1205*
Illinois	Available if gross value of deceased person's real and personal property subject to probate in Illinois does not exceed $100,000. All heirs and beneficiaries must consent in writing. *755 Ill. Comp. Stat. § 5/9-8*
Indiana	Available if value of deceased person's property subject to probate does not exceed $25,000. *Ind. Code Ann. §§ 29-1-8-3 and following*
Iowa	1. If deceased person is survived by a spouse or child: Available if gross value of property subject to Iowa jurisdiction (basically, everything but real estate outside Iowa) doesn't exceed $50,000. 2. If deceased person is survived by parents or grandchildren: Available if gross value of property subject to Iowa jurisdiction (basically, everything but real estate outside Iowa) doesn't exceed $15,000.

STATE	SIMPLIFIED COURT PROCEDURE (cont.)
Iowa (cont.)	3. If deceased person is survived by more distant relatives: Available if gross value of property subject to Iowa jurisdiction (basically, everything but real estate outside Iowa) doesn't exceed $10,000. *Iowa Code § 635.1*
Kansas	"Simplified estate" procedure available if court approves it, based on size of estate, wishes of heirs, and other factors. *Kan. Stat. Ann. §§ 59-3202 and following*
Kentucky	No probate necessary if there is a surviving spouse and value of decedent's property subject to probate is $15,000 or less, or if there is no surviving spouse and someone else has paid at least $15,000 in preferred claims. *Ky. Rev. Stat. Ann. §§ 391.030, 395.455*
Louisiana	This book doesn't cover Louisiana law.
Maine	Available if value of the entire estate, less liens and encumbrances, does not exceed homestead allowance, exempt property, family allowance, costs of administration, reasonable funeral expenses, and reasonable medical expenses of the last illness. *Me. Rev. Stat. Ann. tit.18-A, § 3-1203*
Maryland	Simplified probate is available if property subject to probate in Maryland has a value of $30,000 or less, or if surviving spouse is the only beneficiary, $50,000 or less. *Md. Code Ann. [Est. and Trusts] §§ 5-601 and following*
Massachusetts	Available if estate doesn't exceed $15,000 in value and doesn't include real estate. Executor named in will, or close relative who is Massachusetts resident, may file form with probate court. *Mass. Gen. Laws ch. 195, §§ 16, 16A*

STATE	SIMPLIFIED COURT PROCEDURE (cont.)
Michigan	1. Available if value of decedent's gross estate, after payment of funeral and burial costs, is $15,000 or less. Court can order property turned over to surviving spouse or heirs. *Mich. Comp. Laws § 700.3982*
	2. Available if value of entire estate, less liens and encumbrances, does not exceed homestead allowance, family allowance, exempt property, costs of administration, and reasonable expenses of last illness and funeral. *Mich. Comp. Laws § 700.3987*
Minnesota	If court determines that no property is subject to creditors' claims (because it is exempt from claims or must be set aside for the spouse and children), can order estate closed without further proceedings. *Minn. Stat. Ann. § 524.3-1203*
Mississippi	Available if value of estate is $500 or less. *Miss. Code Ann. § 91-7-147*
Missouri	Available if value of the entire estate, less liens and encumbrances, is $40,000 or less. *Mo. Rev. Stat. § 473.097*
Montana	Available if value of entire estate, less liens and encumbrances, doesn't exceed homestead allowance, exempt property, family allowance, costs of administration, funeral expenses, and medical expenses of the last illness. *Mont. Code Ann. § 72-3-1103*
Nebraska	Available if value of entire estate, less liens and encumbrances, doesn't exceed homestead allowance, exempt property, family allowance, costs of administration, funeral expenses, and medical expenses of the last illness. *Neb. Rev. Stat. § 30-24, 127*
Nevada	1. Available if gross value of estate doesn't exceed $200,000, if court approves. *Nev. Rev. Stat. Ann. §§ 145.020 and following*

STATE	SIMPLIFIED COURT PROCEDURE (cont.)
Nevada (cont.)	2. Available if gross value of estate, less encumbrances, doesn't exceed $75,000. Court can set aside all property for surviving spouse or minor children, or if there are neither, to pay debts. *Nev. Rev. Stat. Ann. § 146.070*
New Hampshire	Available if deceased person owned no real estate and gross value of all property doesn't exceed $10,000. *N.H. Rev. Stat. Ann. § 553:31*
New Jersey	Two procedures, available only if there is no valid will:
	1. If value of all property doesn't exceed $20,000, surviving spouse is entitled to all of it without probate. *N.J. Stat. Ann. § 3B:10-3*
	2. If value of all property doesn't exceed $10,000 and there is no surviving spouse, one heir, with the written consent of the others, can file affidavit with the court and receive all the assets. *N.J. Stat. Ann. § 3B:10-4*
New Mexico	Available if value of entire estate, less liens and encumbrances, doesn't exceed personal property allowance, family allowance, costs of administration, funeral expenses, and medical expenses of the last illness. *N.M. Stat. Ann. § 45-3-1203*
New York	Available if property, excluding real estate and amounts that must be set aside for surviving family members, has a gross value of $20,000 or less. *N.Y. Surr. Ct. Proc. Act Law § 1301*
North Carolina	None
North Dakota	Available if value of the entire estate, less liens and encumbrances, does not exceed the homestead, plus exempt property, family allowance, costs of administration, funeral expenses, and medical expenses of the last illness. *N.D. Cent. Code § 30.1-23-03*

STATE	SIMPLIFIED COURT PROCEDURE (cont.)
Ohio	Available if either: • value of the estate is $35,000 or less, or • surviving spouse inherits everything, either under a will or by law, and value of the estate is $100,000 or less. *Ohio Rev. Code Ann. § 2113.03*
Oklahoma	Available if value of estate is $150,000 or less. *Okla. Stat. Ann. tit. 58, § 241*
Oregon	Available if fair market value of the estate is $140,000 or less, and not more than $50,000 of the estate is personal property and not more than $90,000 is real estate. *Or. Rev. Stat. §§ 114.505 and following*
Pennsylvania	Available if property (not counting real estate, certain payments the family is entitled to, and funeral costs) is worth $25,000 or less. *20 Pa. Cons. Stat. Ann. § 3102*
Rhode Island	Available if deceased person owned no real estate, and value of property that would be subject to probate (not counting tangible personal property) doesn't exceed $15,000. Executor or certain relatives, if resident of state, can file statement on form prescribed by court. *R.I. Gen. Laws § 33-24-1*
South Carolina	Available if value of property passing by will or under law, less liens and encumbrances, is $10,000 or less (not counting exempt property, funeral expenses, and medical expenses of last illness). *S.C. Code Ann. § 62-3-1203*
South Dakota	"Informal probate" available regardless of value of estate. *S.D. Codified Laws Ann. §§ 29A-3-301 and following*
Tennessee	Available if value of property, not counting property held jointly with right of survivorship or real estate, is $25,000 or less. *Tenn. Code Ann. §§ 30-4-102 and following*

STATE	SIMPLIFIED COURT PROCEDURE (cont.)
Texas	1. Available if value of property doesn't exceed that needed to pay family allowance and certain creditors. *Tex. Prob. Code Ann. § 143* 2. "Independent administration" available, regardless of value of estate, if requested in the will or all inheritors agree to it. *Tex. Prob. Code Ann. § 145*
Utah	Available if value of the entire estate, less liens and encumbrances, does not exceed the homestead allowance, exempt property, family allowance, costs of administration, funeral expenses, and medical expenses of the last illness. *Utah Code Ann. § 75-3-1203*
Vermont	Available if the deceased is survived by a spouse or children and owned no real estate, and the value of the personal property is $10,000 or less. *Vt. Stat. Ann., tit. 14, § 1902*
Virginia	None
Washington	Available for solvent estates of any size. *Wash. Rev. Code Ann. §§ 11.68.011 and following*
West Virginia	Available if value of estate, not counting real estate, is $100,000 or less; or if the personal representative is the sole beneficiary of the estate; or if the surviving spouse is the sole beneficiary of the estate; or if all the beneficiaries state that no disputes are likely, there are enough assets to pay debts and taxes and the executor agrees. *W. Va. Code § 44-3A-5*
Wisconsin	Available if value of estate, less mortgages and encumbrances, is $50,000 or less and the decedent is survived by a spouse or minor children. *Wis. Stat. Ann. § 867.01*. Also available if value of estate, less mortgages and encumbrances, does not exceed costs, expenses, allowances, and claims.
Wyoming	Available if value of entire estate including real estate and mineral interests is $150,000 or less. *Wyo. Stat. § 2-1-205*

■

CHAPTER 9

Make Gifts

Giving away property while you're alive is very different from the other probate-avoidance strategies in this book, which all involve leaving things to people at your death. For one, gifts made during life are generous in a way that gifts at death can never be. After all, it's no sacrifice to part with things only when you cannot—beyond a doubt— use them anymore. Making gifts requires you to give up something now. In return, it gives you the joy of watching your gifts help people you love or organizations you admire.

Making gifts helps you avoid probate for a very simple reason: If you don't own something when you die, it doesn't have to go through probate. That lowers probate costs because, as a general rule, the higher the monetary value of the assets that go through probate, the higher the expense. If you give away enough assets, your estate might even qualify for a streamlined "small estate" probate procedure after your death. (See Chapter 8.)

All you need to make a gift is a checkbook; no fancy documents (or legal fees) are required. But before you embark on a gift-giving program, you should understand a little about federal gift tax. Sorry.

GIFT-GIVING AT A GLANCE

Pros

- It's easy to do.
- You get to see your gifts enjoyed by the recipients.
- Giving property away saves estate taxes, if your estate will be large enough to be subject to them.

Cons

- Once you give property away, it's gone for good.
- Large gifts—currently, more than $12,000 per recipient per year— require a federal gift tax return and may be subject to tax.
- Gifts to minors are subject to special rules to keep their tax-free status.

A. The Federal Gift Tax

Making large gifts is usually a tax-saving strategy, not a probate-avoidance one. Wealthy people give away property so that when they die, there will be less property to tax. The tax that the givers are trying to reduce or eliminate is the federal "unified gift and estate tax."

Estate tax is a concern for very few Americans. Legislation passed in 2001 drastically changed the entire estate and gift tax system, eliminating the tax for all but the wealthiest citizens. For deaths in 2006, 2007, or 2008, the gift and estate tax kicks in if:

- during your life, you give away more than $1 million in taxable gifts (many kinds of gifts are tax-free, as discussed below), or

- at your death, the value of the taxable property you leave behind (property left to your spouse or a tax-exempt charity isn't taxable) plus taxable gifts you made during life, is more than $2 million.

The individual exemption amount is scheduled to increase until the estate tax goes away entirely in 2010. Unless Congress extends the repeal, however, the estate tax will reappear in 2011.

If the estate tax repeal happens on schedule, the gift tax will survive, but everyone will get a $1 million exemption. So unless you plan to make at least $1 million in taxable gifts (and most ordinary gifts are not taxable), gift tax will not be worth a second thought.

The estate tax is a highly charged political issue. Look for Congress to take up the subject again before 2010.

HOW THE ESTATE TAX WILL FADE AWAY

Year	Estate tax exemption	Gift tax exemption	Highest estate and gift tax rate
2006	$2 million	$1 million	46%
2007	$2 million	$1 million	45%
2008	$2 million	$1 million	45%
2009	$3.5 million	$1 million	45%
2010	Estate tax repealed	$1 million	top individual income tax rate (gift tax only)

Why worry about gift and estate taxes at all if you don't ever expect your net worth to cross the estate tax threshold? One reason is that if you make large gifts—currently, more than $12,000 to one recipient in one calendar year—federal law requires you to file a gift tax return, even though you may never owe a penny of tax.

If you are concerned about gift and estate taxes, get more information. Especially given the uncertainty surrounding gift and estate tax, you'll need to educate yourself. You may want to start with *Plan Your Estate*, by Denis Clifford and Cora Jordan, also published by Nolo.

B. Making Tax-Free Gifts

Many kinds of gifts are exempt from gift tax. If you structure your gifts properly and watch the calendar, you can probably give away as much money as you want without worrying about tax.

All these gifts are exempt from federal gift tax:

- gifts of up to $12,000 per any recipient per year (this amount is éí‰Uxed for inflation)
- direct payment of someone's tuition or medical bills
- gifts of any amount to your spouse, and
- donations of any amount to tax-exempt charities.

1. Gifts of Up to the Annual Exclusion Amount

Federal tax law contains a blanket exemption from gift tax for all gifts worth no more than $12,000. (This figure is indexed for inflation and will eventually go up.) You can give any number of recipients up to the exempt amount in gifts each calendar year without needing to file a gift tax return. (26 U.S.C. §§ 2503(b), 6019.)

If you're determined to give away lots of money, you can probably stretch this exemption (or exclusion, as the IRS calls it) into a lot more. For example, if you're part of a couple, and are used to thinking of your money together with your mate's, the two of you together have twice the annual exemption per recipient. In fact, even if only one spouse makes a gift, it's considered to have been made by both spouses if they both consent. (26 U.S.C. § 2513.) If you give money to another couple, there's $48,000 tax-free the first year.

Example: *Joe and Faye, a couple in their late 70s, want to give their son and his wife money for a down payment on a house. They also see this as an opportunity to get some money out of their estate and reduce the probate and tax bills their son—who will inherit everything anyway—will eventually have to pay.*

Both Joe and Faye take advantage of their annual exemption to give a total of $24,000 to their son and another $24,000 to his wife. As soon as the first of the year rolls around, they can give away that much again if they're still feeling well-off and altruistic.

You can make the most of the annual exemption if you keep in mind that it is all based on a calendar year. If you miss a year, you can't go back and claim the exclusion. But if you spread a large gift over two or more years, you may escape gift tax complications.

Example: *If you give your daughter $20,000 on December 17, $8,000 of that gift is taxable. You'll have to file a gift tax return (by April 15 of the next year) and you'll have used up $8,000 of the total you're allowed to give away or leave tax-free.*

But if you give her only $10,000 in December, and wait a couple of weeks before handing over the other $10,000 on January 1, both gifts are tax-free, and no gift tax return is required.

Not only cash can be split. Give some stocks now, some next year. You can even give real estate in pieces—physical pieces, if that's possible, or pieces of ownership. (For a discussion of what kind of property makes a good gift—from a tax standpoint—see Section D, below.)

Example: *Solomon and his wife Rhoda want to give their vacation cabin to their son Gerard. The cabin is worth $75,000, but their equity is only $40,000; there is still $35,000 left to pay on the mortgage. In November, Solomon and Rhoda sign a deed transferring the house to Rhoda and Gerard as joint tenants. That means that Rhoda and Gerard each own a ½ interest in the property. Gerard's share is worth $20,000; the gift from his parents is tax-free because together, they can give him up to $24,000 tax-free each calendar year.*

The next calendar year, Rhoda gives her half-share, worth $20,000 to Gerard. Even though only Rhoda makes the gift, the IRS considers it, for tax purposes, to have come from both spouses.

Ingenious taxpayers (and their lawyers) have come up with all sorts of ways to make the annual exemption work overtime for them. But it's best not to try to get too fancy. Section C, below, discusses some schemes that may backfire.

⚠️ **Special rules apply when you make tax-free gifts to children.** Gifts to minors must be structured so as not to run afoul of IRS rules. See Section E, below.

2. Gifts for Tuition or Medical Bills

If you pay someone else's tuition or medical bills, the government does not tax your generosity, no matter how great. (26 U.S.C. § 2503(e).)

One very important rule applies: The money must be paid directly to the school or the provider of medical services. If, for example, you write your granddaughter a check for tuition, and she in turn writes a check to the college from her account for exactly the same amount, the gift is not tax-free under this provision. It will be tax-free, of course, if you give her no more than the annual exclusion amount during the calendar year. (With that in mind, you may want to remind the youngsters in your family of the excellent education available at many public universities.) Similarly, if you reimburse someone who has already paid a medical bill, your gift is not tax-free.

Federal law limits what expenses are covered. Here are the rules:

Tuition. Tuition means just that: what a school charges for education or training. You cannot make tax-free gifts for lodging, books, or supplies. The tuition exemption is not, by any means, limited to higher or even academic education. Tuition can be paid to any "educational organization" that has a "regular faculty and curriculum" and a regularly enrolled body of students "in attendance where its educational activities are regularly carried on." (26 U.S.C. §§ 170, 2503(e).) That definition seems to include just about every kind of school except correspondence schools and mail-order diploma mills.

Medical bills. You can pay, gift-tax free, for:

- the diagnosis, treatment, or prevention of disease
- transportation primarily for and essential to these kinds of medical care
- insurance (including supplementary medical insurance for the aged) covering these kinds of medical care, or
- lodging of up to $50/night for each individual (as long as it's not "lavish or extravagant under the circumstances," which seems unlikely to be a problem at $50 a night) while away from home, if it's essential to the medical care, if the medical care is provided by a physician in a licensed hospital (or a facility that is related to, or the equivalent of, a licensed hospital), and there is no significant element of personal pleasure in the travel. (26 U.S.C. § 213.)

Cosmetic surgery and similar procedures aren't covered, unless they are necessary because of a disfiguring illness or injury.

3. Gifts to Your Spouse

All gifts that you make to your spouse are tax-free, as long as he or she is a U.S. citizen. If your spouse isn't a citizen, the limit on tax-free gifts is currently $120,000 per year. This amount is indexed for inflation. (26 U.S.C. § 2523(a).)

In practice, there's rarely much of a reason to make large gifts to your spouse. You could actually worsen your tax situation by saddling your spouse with an estate that's so large it will be taxed at his or her death.

4. Gifts to Charities

If you would like to donate to a charity, the federal government will smile on you. All gifts to tax-exempt charities are exempt from gift tax. (26 U.S.C. § 2522.) If you aren't sure whether or not an organization to which you wish to contribute is tax-exempt, just ask a staffer there; someone will be more than happy to help you.

Many people simply write checks to a favorite charity. But if you want to make very large gifts and are concerned about gift and estate tax, you may want to consider a different method, involving what's called a charitable trust. In addition to benefiting the charity, it could provide you with income while you're alive and reduce your eventual estate taxes.

CHARITY BEGINS WITH A TRUST

There are many varieties of charitable trusts. The most common kind, called a charitable remainder trust, works like this: You set up a trust while you are alive, and make an irrevocable gift of property (cash, stocks, or real estate, for example) to it. The charity manages the trust property and distributes a certain part of the income it generates to you or to someone else you've chosen. At your death, the property goes to the charity; because it belonged to the trust, not to you, your estate is not liable for estate tax on it.

For detailed information about different kinds of charitable trusts, see *Plan Your Estate*, by Denis Clifford and Cora Jordan (Nolo).

C. Gifts That Could Land You in Tax Trouble

It's the IRS's job to look for estate planning strategies that cross the line from clever to forbidden. Here are a few gift-giving strategies frowned on by the feds. Even if you're not making gifts in order to save on gift and estate tax, you don't want to inadvertently stir up a gift tax problem.

1. Loans That Are Really Gifts

Some parents have made large loans to their children, intending to forgive the repayments each year, in an amount equal to the annual gift tax exclusion amount. The IRS, skeptical of these arrangements to start with, makes it difficult for families to prove that they are bona fide loans, not gifts in disguise. But the bottom line seems to be that if you are meticulous about your paperwork, this strategy can be successful.

The IRS starts with the presumption that a transfer between family members is a gift. You can get around that presumption by showing that you really expected repayment and intended to enforce the debt. In making that determination, the IRS pays attention to whether or not:

- The borrower signed a promissory note.
- You charged interest.
- There was security (collateral) for the debt.
- You demanded repayment.
- The borrower actually repaid some of the loan.
- There was a fixed date that the loan was due to be repaid.
- The borrower had the ability to repay.
- Your records or those of the recipient indicated that the transfer was a loan.
- The transaction was reported, for federal tax purposes, as a loan.

In the case that prompted this slew of considerations, a woman had loaned $100,000 to each of her two sons. They signed promissory notes, and the loans were duly recorded in the books of the family's business, but there was no deadline for repayment. One of the sons made a $15,000 repayment. Their mother never demanded any payments, and each year she sent a letter to the sons, stating that she had forgiven (canceled) some of the debt. The IRS ruled, and the federal Tax Court agreed, that the loans had actually been gifts. The mother ended up not only owing gift tax on the whole amount, but missing out on the years when she could have been (and thought she was) making tax-free annual gifts. (*Elizabeth B. Miller*, Tax Court Memo 1996-3.)

Don't try this yourself. If you want to set up an elaborate scheme for forgiving debts, form is everything. See a lawyer who's experienced in setting up such deals so that they pass IRS scrutiny.

2. Gifts Made to One Person But Intended for Another

The IRS won't be fooled if you give property to one person but it's obvious that the intended recipient is someone else. For example, the IRS went after the estate of a man who had given annual gifts of stock to his son, daughter-in-law, and grandchildren, classifying each gift as exempt because of the annual gift tax exclusion. For 14 years, the daughter-in-law had faithfully transferred her stock to her husband on the same day she received it. The IRS ruled that the stock was really for the son, and that the gifts to him had exceeded the annual exclusion amount. (*Estate of Joseph Cidulka*, Tax Court Memo 1996-149.)

The gift tax problem doesn't affect the probate-avoidance aspect of the transaction—the stock was out of the man's estate. But shaving a little off your probate costs may be much more trouble than it's worth if it lands you in a skirmish with the IRS.

3. Gifts With Strings Attached

If you give it, give it. Don't try to hang onto any control over what you've given away, or you'll turn your gift into something else.

Example: *Carl deeds his house over to his son, Ishmael, but retains the right to receive rent from the property. The transaction is not a legal gift. When Carl dies, the house will still be part of his estate, which means it may be subject to estate tax.*

Make a paper trail. If you think a gift might be questioned later, write up and sign a little statement that explains your intent to make a gift. It will be evidence that you meant to make a gift, if that's ever needed. Such a statement can't turn what is really a loan into a gift, and other evidence may contradict and finally outweigh it—but it can't hurt.

D. What to Give

Like everything else connected with gift-giving, the kind of property you choose to give away—for example, cash, stocks, or real estate—can have tax consequences for you and for the recipient.

You can give only what's yours. If you own property together with your spouse or someone else, you must both consent before you give it away. Especially in community property states (Arizona, California, Idaho, Louisiana, Nevada, New Mexico, Texas, Washington, and Wisconsin), it can be difficult for married people to know who owns what. See Chapter 6, Section D, if you're unsure about community property rules.

1. Property That Is Likely to Increase in Value

If you're trying to decide what you want to give away, look among your assets for property that you expect to go up in value. If you hold onto it until your death, your estate will be worth that much more, and probate fees (and estate taxes, if your estate is large enough) will be correspondingly higher.

Even if giving away property now is a taxable gift (meaning that some of your personal estate tax exemption will be used up), it may be worth it. Remember that you don't have to actually pay gift and estate tax until you give away or leave more than the exemption amount.

2. Property That Has Increased in Value

It's usually a poor idea, financially speaking, to give away property that has gone up substantially in value since you acquired it. The reason lies, of course, in the tax code.

When you give someone property, the recipient's tax basis—the amount from which taxable profit or loss is calculated if the property is ever sold—is the same as yours.

Example: *Years ago, Vinny paid $100,000 for a piece of land. That amount is his tax basis. Now he gives the land to his niece, Jackie; her tax basis is $100,000, too. If the land is actually worth $150,000 now, and Jackie turns around and sells it, she'll have to pay capital gains tax on her $50,000 gain.*

If, on the other hand, you leave property at your death, a different rule applies. The recipient's tax basis is the market value of the property at the date of your death. In short, if the property has increased in value since you bought it, the recipient will get a higher basis—which translates into lower taxes down the line.

Example: *If Vinny's niece inherits the land from him, her tax basis will be the market value of the property at the time of his death—whether it's more or less than his basis. If the value is still $150,000 when Vinny dies, and Jackie sells the land for that amount, she'll have zero taxable gain.*

Obviously, how these rules should affect your actions depends on your particular situation. If you want to make a gift of appreciated property now and expect to live another 25 years, you won't want to postpone the transfer until your death just for some hypothetical income tax savings.

Different rules apply to charities. There's an important exception to the rule that it's often a bad idea to give away appreciated property: When you're giving to charities, it can be to your financial advantage to donate appreciated property, especially if you're concerned about estate tax. See *Plan Your Estate*, by Denis Clifford and Cora Jordan (Nolo).

E. Gifts to Children

Children are the natural objects of their adult relatives' affection and generosity. But giving them valuable property before they are adults in the eyes of the law involves several special considerations.

1. Who Will Manage the Property?

Minors (in most states, children younger than 18) are not permitted to manage valuable property by themselves; an adult must be responsible. The ceiling varies from state to state, but minors commonly can't own more than a few thousand dollars without adult control.

Fortunately, it's quite easy to choose an adult to manage the property. You can arrange it by setting up either:

- a trust, or
- a custodianship under the Uniform Transfers to Minors Act or the Uniform Gifts to Minors Act.

The easier way is to name an adult to serve as "custodian" of the money. Custodians are authorized under a law called the Uniform Transfers to Minors Act (UTMA) or the Uniform Gifts to Minors Act, one of which has been adopted by every state.

All you need to do is give the property to the adult you choose to be the custodian, instead of to the child directly. The custodian has the legal responsibility to manage and use the money for the benefit of the child. When the child reaches adulthood, the custodian turns over what's left to the beneficiary. In most states, the law requires the property to be turned over to the recipient at 21; in a few states, the age is 18.

Example: *Sam wants to give each of his four young grandchildren $10,000. He names each child's parent as custodian of the money, and the parents open bank accounts as custodians under the state's Uniform Transfers to Minors Act. They will manage the money until the children turn 21.*

STATE LAW DIFFERENCES

All but two states (South Carolina and Vermont) have adopted the Uniform Transfers to Minors Act, which allows you to name a custodian for property that you give to a minor now or that you leave at your death. The ages at which the custodianships must end in each state are listed in Chapter 1, Section C.

The remaining states still have an older law, called the Uniform Gifts to Minors Act, on the books. It authorizes custodians only for gifts made during life, and provides that the custodianship must end when the minor turns 21. The Act also limits the kinds of property that can be given; only money, securities, life insurance policies, and annuity contracts are permitted.

2. Special Gift Tax Rules

You must be careful if you want to give a tax-free gift to a young beneficiary. It's fine to set up a trust or custodianship (discussed just above) to handle the property for the minor. (Rev. Rul. 59-357, 1959-2.) But to qualify for the annual exclusion, the gift must satisfy these conditions:

- The property and its income may be spent by, or for the benefit of, a recipient who isn't 21 yet. You can give the trustee or custodian authority to decide how much of the income or property should be spent, but you can't limit his or her discretion too strictly.

- The recipient must receive the property outright by age 21. This means that if you create a trust for the recipient, the trust document must state that the property will be turned over to the recipient by his or her 21st birthday. (You may, however, give the recipient the right to extend the trust for a longer period.) Similarly, if you set up a custodianship, it must end when the recipient turns 21. Some states allow a custodianship to last until the beneficiary is older than 21; don't choose this option if you're concerned about gift tax.

- If the recipient dies before age 21, the remaining property must be payable to the recipient's estate or to someone the recipient named. (26 U.S.C. § 2503(c).)

3. Income Tax Considerations

Chances are that a minor to whom you make gifts is in a lower income tax bracket than you are. So, if you give income-producing property (stocks, for example) to a minor, he or she will probably pay less tax on the income produced than you would have. But there's an important exception to this rule. If a gift provides a child younger than 14 with annual income of more than $850, the amount over $850 is taxed at his or her parents' highest income tax rate. (26 U.S.C. § 1(g).)

F. Thinking Before You Give

Gift-giving is such an easy and effective way to save on estate taxes that *Fortune* magazine once gushed that it was one of the "Three Things Everyone Should Do Now" to avoid taxes. ("How to Leave the Tax Man Nothing," Mar. 18, 1996.) In fact, an ambitious program of gifts is *not* for everyone. And that goes double if your primary financial motivation is probate avoidance, not estate tax savings.

Start with the obvious: When you give something away, it's gone forever. You can't change your mind. For many people, especially as they get older, shedding material things brings a wonderful sense of lightness and freedom. Add to that the pleasure of seeing a younger relative, friend, or organization benefit from a gift, and giving can return great satisfaction. But if parting with assets makes you feel vulnerable or nervous, fearful that you will someday be without money you need, don't do it.

These decisions are intensely personal. No formula (or lawyer) can tell you how much wealth you need to be comfortable in your own mind and heart. If you feel torn, it may help you to sit down with pencil and paper (or computer) and make rough estimates of your current assets, future income, and expenses, to get a clearer picture of your actual financial situation.

Looking ahead. For a sound discussion of how to estimate your retirement income and expenses realistically, see *Get a Life: You Don't Need a Million to Retire Well*, by Ralph Warner (Nolo).

■

CHAPTER 10

Putting It All Together

Taken one at a time, the probate-avoidance methods discussed in this book are fairly simple. Still, you may feel a little flummoxed when it's actually time to choose among them and take steps to avoid probate for your assets.

This chapter looks at people in several different life situations and what kinds of probate-avoidance strategies work for them. Of course, everyone's situation is unique; your concerns won't match up perfectly with any of the hypothetical people discussed here. But you'll probably spot enough similarities to get some ideas about where to start.

A reminder: This chapter, like the rest of the book, discusses only planning to avoid probate. It doesn't tackle estate tax, incapacity, or other estate planning issues.

Alice and Frank: A Simple Life

Alice and Frank have always worked hard and have much to show for it: a comfortable home in a small Indiana town, four grown children of whom they are very proud, good friends. What they don't have is a lot of material wealth. Now in their late 60s and retired, they live on Alice's modest company pension, withdrawals from Frank's IRA, and their Social Security payments.

They've always figured that they didn't have enough money to concern themselves with estate planning, especially fancy trusts and the like. They do have straightforward wills, which leave their possessions to each other. The wills name their children as alternate beneficiaries; they'll inherit everything, in equal shares, after both Alice and Frank have died. But Alice and Frank want the kids to inherit their property without needless legal fees, delay, or hassles. That prompts them to look into some simple probate-avoidance techniques.

The house. The couple's most valuable asset is their house. It's long since paid for, and is probably worth about $75,000.

The deed to the property shows that Alice and Frank own it in tenancy by the entirety, a version of joint tenancy limited to married couples. That takes care of probate when the first spouse dies; when that happens, the survivor will own it, without probate. Alice and Frank discuss putting the house in joint tenancy with the children, but decide against it. They love their children, but just don't feel completely comfortable giving away ownership rights in the house.

They decide, finally, to make a simple living trust, and transfer only their house to it. They name all the children as beneficiaries, and their daughter Nancy as successor trustee. They've already named her to be executor of their wills. It will fall to her, as successor trustee, to transfer ownership of the house to all the children after both parents have died.

Bank accounts. Aside from the house, the couple's main asset is a savings account. It's held in joint tenancy with the right of survivorship. That means that when Frank or Alice dies, the survivor will automatically own the entire account, without probate. Alice and Frank could transfer the account to their living trust, but decide it's even easier to make their children payable-on-death (P.O.D.) payees for the account, so that when the survivor dies, any remaining funds will go directly to the children, again without probate.

They go to the bank, where a clerk gives them a short form to fill out. Then they list their children's names as the payable-on-death beneficiaries, sign the form, and give it back to the clerk. While they're at it, they do the same thing with their joint checking account. It doesn't have a lot of money in it, but that's all the more reason, they decide, to make sure it doesn't have to get tangled up in probate. The whole process takes ten minutes and costs nothing.

Frank's IRA. On a form provided by the bank that handles his IRA, Frank has already named Alice as the beneficiary for this account. If he dies first, she'll inherit the money. If she dies before he does, the children are named as alternates. No probate will be necessary.

Alice and Frank decide that this is all the probate-avoidance planning they need. The rest of their property, which they'll leave through their wills, should fall below the $25,000 cutoff for "small estates" under Indiana law. That means that it will qualify for simplified transfer procedures, which shouldn't be expensive or burdensome for the children.

ALICE AND FRANK'S PROBATE-AVOIDANCE PLAN

Asset	Plan
House	Change from tenancy by the entirety to a simple living trust.
Bank accounts	Keep in joint tenancy; also name payable-on-death beneficiaries, to inherit the funds after both parents have died.
Frank's IRA	No action needed; Frank has already named a beneficiary, on a form provided by the bank that administers his IRA account.
Everything else (car, household belongings)	Leave to each other by will. Should pass under Indiana simplified "small estate" procedures.

Maria: Dealing With Widowhood

Maria is an Illinois widow in her 70s with a son and daughter in their 40s and two grandchildren, her son's children. When her husband died six years ago, she inherited everything he owned. Their house had been held in joint tenancy, and was easy to transfer into her name after his death. Other assets, however, had to go through probate. Maria found the process confusing, tiring, and expensive. She is determined to spare her two children the burden of probate, as much as is reasonably possible, at her death.

To that end, she takes a quick inventory of her property. The most valuable asset is the house, which has risen to $350,000 in value. The mortgage has been paid in full. She also owns two sizable mutual fund accounts, some IBM stock, some certificates of deposit at her bank, and a checking account. Some of Maria's other possessions aren't particularly economically valuable, but they are precious to her: a collection of stamps that she wants her grandson to inherit and the family china that she wants to pass on to her daughter.

Maria's will was written 15 years ago, while her husband was alive and before their grandchildren were born. It leaves her entire estate to him, with their son and daughter as alternate beneficiaries. It would still work to pass her property to her children, but everything would have to go through probate, and it wouldn't leave the china or stamps to the people she now has in mind. Maria decides she would like both to avoid probate and fine-tune the way she leaves her property.

Bank accounts. First, Maria tackles the easy things. The bank accounts and CDs are quickly turned into payable-on-death accounts, with her son and daughter as the P.O.D. beneficiaries. The bank provides the form; all Maria has to do is list their names. The bank confirms that all the payees will have to do, to collect the funds after Maria's death, is present a copy of her death certificate, and identification, to the bank.

Stocks and mutual fund accounts. The stock accounts are also simple to handle, although the paperwork takes a bit longer. Because she lives in Illinois, which allows transfer-on-death registration of securities, she can simply reregister her ownership in transfer-on-death (T.O.D.) form. Like the P.O.D. bank accounts, stock held this way will pass without probate to the beneficiaries she names.

Maria calls the mutual fund company and explains that she wants to register her ownership in transfer-on-death form. The company sends her a form to fill out, on which she lists her son and daughter as beneficiaries.

Maria also reregisters the IBM stock; her broker contacts the company's transfer agent to get the paperwork. But she wants her son's children, who are both minors, to inherit this stock. So she names as beneficiary her son, as "custodian" for each of the grandchildren, under the Illinois Uniform Transfers to Minors Act. That way if the grandchildren inherit the stock before they turn 21, their father will manage it for them. (The Uniform Transfers to Minors Act is explained in Chapter 1.)

The house. Maria decides that a living trust is the best way to avoid probate for her house. So she creates a trust and signs a new deed, transferring the house to herself as trustee of her living trust. She names her children as the trust beneficiaries.

Heirlooms. Beause she's created a living trust, Maria decides to use it to leave some heirlooms—the stamp collection, set of china, and a few others, so they won't have to go through probate. So in the trust document, she leaves the stamps to her grandson, the china to her daughter, and a few other items to her son.

The car. Maria's car is an old Mercedes that her son has always loved. Maria decides to put her son's name on the title with her, as joint tenants. That way, he will inherit it at her death, without probate. She doesn't worry that giving away a half-interest will cause any problems.

And because the value of the gift she is making is not worth more than $10,000, Maria does not need to file a gift tax return.

The leftovers. Finally, Maria makes a new will. Because she has taken care of almost everything in her trust, the will is short and simple. It says only that anything not specifically left by another method should go to her son and daughter, in equal shares. The will is essentially a back-up device, so that Maria knows that everything is taken care of. And Illinois's special procedures for small estates allow up to $100,000 of property to avoid regular probate.

MARIA'S PROBATE-AVOIDANCE PLAN

Asset	Plan
House	Transfer by living trust.
Bank accounts and CDs	Name payable-on-death beneficiaries.
IBM stock	Register in transfer-on-death (beneficiary) form, naming a custodian to manage the stock if beneficiaries are still minors when they inherit.
Mutual funds	Register in transfer-on-death (beneficiary) form.
Stamp collection, family china	Transfer by living trust.
Car	Put into joint tenancy ownership with son.
Everything else (household belongings)	Pass under will (should qualify for special "small estate" transfer procedure).

Maria adds up the value of all her property. Because it doesn't come close to the estate tax exemption amount (the current amount or the $1 million that is scheduled to reappear in 2011), her children won't have to pay estate tax after her death, and she doesn't need to look into methods of reducing the tax bill.

Mike: Midlife Concerns

Mike is a divorced father who owns a mortgaged house in Wyoming, a growing retirement account, and some other investments. His son, Bryce, is a teenager.

Mike, who is a healthy 50, expects quite reasonably that he will live many more years. But he is by nature a cautious person and wants to make sure that if anything happened to him, his son would be taken care of. And he hates the idea of having 5% of the value of his estate go toward probate costs and fees, when it could go for Bryce's college education instead.

The house. Mike's most valuable asset, by far, is his house. It's worth about $80,000; his equity is about $25,000. He considers making a living trust to avoid probate, but is reluctant; after all, he probably won't even own this house in 25 years' time, when death will be closer. He is delighted to find that under Wyoming law, simplified probate is available for real estate if the entire estate is valued at $150,000 or less. So, if the unexpected does happen, probate shouldn't be onerous—his executor should only have to file a few papers. He crosses the house off his list.

Retirement plan funds. This one is easy, too. Mike has named his son Bryce as beneficiary of his 401(k) retirement plan. But because he is still younger than 18, Mike has named his ex-wife to be the custodian of the money, under the Wyoming Uniform Transfers to Minors Act. Although he doesn't want to live with her, he trusts her to use the money for the boy they both love. Under the Wyoming law, the money—whatever is left of it—must be turned over to his son when he turns 21.

Bank accounts. Mike decides it can't hurt to make his bank accounts payable on death to Bryce, again with his wife as custodian of the funds. To do this, he just fills out and signs the form the bank teller hands him, naming Bryce as the P.O.D. payee. He knows that Bryce won't have any claim to the money now, but will receive it when Mike dies.

He follows essentially the same procedure to put his mutual fund accounts in transfer-on-death form, with Bryce as the beneficiary. He can do so because Wyoming has adopted the Uniform Transfer-on-Death Security Registration Act. (See Chapter 3.)

The car. Mike owns a nice car, one that's still worth a fair amount of money though it's three years old. But even a man of his pronounced cautiousness is sure that he will be around long after the car is rusting and abandoned. He decides not to worry about planning to avoid probate of the car.

Life insurance. Mike's main estate planning concern, at this stage of his life, isn't actually probate avoidance: it's making sure that if he died prematurely, his son would be provided for through college. So he also buys some term life insurance, naming Bryce as beneficiary, to replace the income he would have used to support Bryce. Because a life insurance policy is a contract between company and customer, the company pays the proceeds directly to the beneficiary, without probate.

Leftovers. Finally, Mike makes a brief will. He leaves everything to his son except for some small gifts to charity. He also names his sister as Bryce's personal guardian, who would look after his son in the extremely unlikely event that both Mike and his ex-wife died before Bryce reached 18. Although the items left by the will would have to go through probate, Mike realizes that this probably isn't the last will he'll make; he's using it more as a backup device than a definitive plan. If he later acquires more valuable property, setting up a probate-avoidance living trust may become justified.

MIKE'S PROBATE-AVOIDANCE PLAN

Asset	Plan
House	Pass by simplified probate.
401(k) plan	Name beneficiary on form provided by plan administrator.
Bank accounts	Name payable-on-death beneficiary.
Mutual funds	Put in transfer-on-death registration.
Car	Leave by will (doesn't avoid probate).
Everything else (household belongings)	Leave by will (doesn't avoid probate).

Jim and Terry: An Unmarried Couple

Estate planning is a bigger concern to Jim and Terry than it is to most other men in their 40s. That's because Jim and Terry are a gay couple, who've been together nine years. Unlike a married person, in most states the surviving member of an unmarried couple does not have any rights to any of the deceased partner's property. (Only California, Connecticut, Hawaii, Maine, and Vermont allow a registered domestic partner to inherit from a deceased partner just as a spouse would, if there is no will.) In the absence of an estate plan, Jim and Terry's closest relatives would inherit their property.

They own two large assets together: their house, which is worth about $375,000, and a mutual fund account. Over the years, they've bought a television, computer, stereo, furniture, and other household items together, too. Each separately owns bank accounts, a car, and a retirement account.

Because they're in good health and relatively young, Jim and Terry don't want to invest a lot of effort in probate avoidance right now. They've been planning just to write basic wills, to be sure that property goes to the surviving partner. But first, they decide to consider some simple probate-avoidance steps—ones that won't take a lot of money or time.

The house. They start by checking the deed to their house—something they haven't looked at since they closed escrow four years ago. They find that the deed lists them as "tenants in common." That means that if one of them died tomorrow, the survivor would not automatically inherit the deceased partner's half-interest.

To solve this problem, they decide to put title to the house into joint tenancy. That way, when one partner dies, the house would automatically belong to the other. And they kill another bird with the same stone: Probate won't be required, either. All they have to do is prepare and sign a new deed, transferring the property from themselves as tenants in common to themselves as "joint tenants with right of survivorship." They record (file) the deed with the county land records office, and they're done.

That takes care of probate at the death of the first partner—but not the second. But Jim and Terry decide that they're just not willing to worry about that now. There should be plenty of time for the survivor to deal with that issue—perhaps by creating a living trust—later.

The mutual fund account. Neither Jim nor Terry can remember how they set up ownership to the mutual fund account they opened together. But when they check their latest account statement, they get a pleasant surprise: They are already joint tenants with right of survivorship—or, as the statement has it, "JT WROS." Nothing to do there.

Bank and retirement accounts. Jim and Terry decide to name each other as the payable-on-death beneficiary of the bank accounts they each own separately. It's easy and free, and again solves two problems: getting the money to the person they want to inherit it and avoiding probate. They do the same thing with their retirement accounts: on the forms provided by the account custodian, they list each other as beneficiary.

Cars, household items, and the like. Jim and Terry deal with the rest of their belongings in their wills. Each leaves his share of household items to the other, and they both also use their wills to leave gifts to family members, friends, and charities.

Those beneficiaries will probably be able to claim their property with a simple affidavit (sworn statement), without any probate court involvement. That's because Jim and Terry live in Colorado, which offers a simple, out-of-court procedure for claiming assets when an estate contains property worth less than $50,000. Many assets—those owned in joint tenancy or held in a living trust, for example—aren't considered when determining whether or not an estate is under the $50,000 cutoff, so the estate of Jim or Terry would probably qualify for the affidavit procedure.

JIM AND TERRY'S PROBATE-AVOIDANCE PLAN

Asset	Plan
House	Put in joint tenancy.
Bank and retirement accounts	Name payable-on-death beneficiaries.
Mutual fund	Keep in joint tenancy.
Cars and everything else	Pass under wills (will probably avoid probate because of Colorado rules for small estates).

Esther and Mark: New Love, Old Money

Esther and Mark met when they were both convinced that they would spend the rest of their lives alone. Esther had divorced after a long marriage; Mark was a widower. But their friendship grew until they realized it wasn't just friendship, it was love. They were married soon after and moved into Esther's home in Connecticut.

Esther has considerable property of her own: the house, which is worth $500,000, stocks and CDs worth another several hundred thousand dollars, and valuable household furnishings. Mark is also quite comfortable financially, with his own small business and considerable savings. He has one grown son from his first marriage. Mark and Esther have kept their property separate for the sake of simplicity.

Esther wants her property, much of which she inherited from her parents, to go to her three daughters. But she doesn't want Mark to think that she's trying to cut him out, and she would want him to keep on living in her house for as long as he wished to after her death. Difficult as it is to talk about these issues, she raises them to Mark. She's immensely relieved to find that he would prefer that she leave her wealth directly to her children, with whom he gets along well. As her husband, he would have the legal right, after her death, to claim a portion of her estate.

Esther's house and other valuable items. Esther wants to give Mark the right to live in the house for the rest of his life, but have her daughters inherit it after his death. A simple probate-avoidance living trust can't do that; she needs a more complicated "AB" trust, which will also avoid probate. (With an AB trust, the surviving spouse gets to use property for life; then, the children inherit the property.) She'll use the trust to transfer other valuable and not-so-valuable items, too, such as household furnishings and art. Another important benefit of an AB trust is that it can save on estate taxes, which Esther's estate may owe, depending on the tax laws in effect when she dies.

Esther's stock and bank accounts. Esther calls her stockbroker and asks about the procedure for naming her children as T.O.D. beneficiaries for her stocks, so they can inherit them without probate. The broker sends her the paperwork. She also fills out a form provided by her bank to name them as P.O.D. payees for her CDs and other accounts.

Mark's business. Mark wants his son David to inherit the family business, a camera store. David already works with Mark managing the business. Mark decides that for the time being, a probate-avoidance living trust is the way to go. He transfers the business assets to a trust, naming David as the beneficiary and successor trustee.

Mark's investments. Mark wants to leave much of his other wealth, in the form of stocks and bonds, to several charities. To avoid probate for these assets, he could name the charities as transfer-on-death beneficiaries of his securities. But because his estate could be large enough to owe estate taxes, Mark plans to talk to the charities about setting up charitable trusts. Such trusts would provide income tax breaks for him while he's alive, and leave more for the charities after his death. The charities will be more than happy to discuss these plans with him.

ESTHER AND MARK'S PROBATE-AVOIDANCE PLAN

Asset	Plan
Esther's house and valuable furnishings	Put in AB living trust to avoid both probate and estate tax and to give Mark rights after Esther's death.
Esther's bank and stock accounts	Name her daughters as payable-on-death beneficiaries.
Esther's leftovers	Leave by will (won't avoid probate).
Mark's small business	Put in living trust to avoid probate (and explore other techniques to avoid estate taxes).
Mark's securities	Name charities as payable-on-death beneficiaries (and explore setting up charitable trusts to save on estate taxes).
Mark's leftovers	Leave by will (won't avoid probate).

More about trusts and taxes. For more information on AB trusts, charitable trusts, and other ways to save on estate taxes, see *Plan Your Estate*, by Denis Clifford and Cora Jordan (Nolo).

Linda and Tomas: Comfortable

Linda and Tomas are a couple in their early 60s with what they think of as a comfortable but far from lavish lifestyle. They bought their home in a California suburb 25 years ago, and it has gone up in value far beyond what they ever expected. They've also managed to amass some savings, which they are depleting to help their two children through college and graduate school. Linda and Tomas have also contributed to company-sponsored retirement plans for many years.

They've never thought much about estate planning. But recently a friend near their age contracted a serious disease, and it got them thinking: Why not take some simple steps that will make things easier on the survivor when one of them eventually dies?

The house. Checking their deed, they find that it lists them as owners of their house "as husband and wife." A little investigating reveals that this wording means that title to the house is held as community property. A little more research, and they learn that in California, they can hold the house "in community property with right of survivorship," giving the survivor automatic ownership of the house. They decide to sign and record a new deed, changing the way they hold title. Later, after one spouse dies, the survivor will be able to create a simple probate-avoidance trust and transfer the house to it. A more cautious couple, concerned about the possibility of simultaneous death, might go ahead and make a trust now, but Linda and Tomas just don't want to bother.

The savings. Linda and Tomas hold their bank and securities accounts in joint tenancy. That means that they don't need to worry about probate when the first spouse dies. Still, they decide to convert the accounts to payable-on-death accounts, so that they can name their son and daughter to inherit after both of them have died. It's easy and doesn't cost anything, and would take effect if they both died at the same time in an accident.

The retirement accounts. Linda and Tomas have already named each other as the primary beneficiary of their retirement accounts. As alternate beneficiaries, they named their children. In case the children inherit while they're still young, they specified that the money would go to a custodian, Linda's brother. He would manage it until each child turned 25, as allowed under California's Uniform Transfers to Minors Act.

Their cars. Linda and Tomas expect to outlive their current vehicles by many years. But after learning that California allows transfer-on-death car registration, they decide to register their next car that way. It's free and simple; all they do is specify the transfer-on-death owner when they register the car.

The leftovers. Linda and Tomas both write simple wills, leaving each other their other items of property. Later, if they amass lots more property, they may make a simple probate-avoidance trust. Because California has a simple small estate procedure, which currently covers estates of less than $100,000, they may decide they don't need a living trust.

LINDA AND TOMAS'S PROBATE-AVOIDANCE PLAN

Asset	Plan
House	Hold as community property with right of survivorship, so it will automatically go to the survivor at the first spouse's death.
Bank accounts	Keep in joint tenancy; also name payable-on-death beneficiaries, to inherit the funds after both parents have died.

LINDA AND TOMAS'S PROBATE-AVOIDANCE PLAN (cont.)

Asset	Plan
Retirement accounts	No action needed; both Linda and Tomas have already named each other as beneficiaries, on a form provided by the plan administrators.
Cars	Register in transfer-on-death form.
Everything else (household belongings)	Leave to each other, with children as alternates, by will. (May not avoid probate; depends on value at the time of death.)

GLOSSARY

Administrator: The person who is appointed by the probate court, when there is no will, to collect assets of the estate, pay its debts, and distribute the rest to the beneficiaries.

Affiant: Someone who signs an affidavit.

Affidavit: A written statement of facts that is signed under oath before a notary public.

Ancillary probate: A probate proceeding conducted in a different state from the one the deceased person resided in at the time of death. Usually, ancillary probate proceedings are necessary if the deceased person owned real estate in another state.

Appraiser: A person who is hired to determine the market value of real estate or other property. Probate courts sometimes appoint an appraiser to place a value on the property in an estate.

Appreciated property: Property that has gone up in value since you acquired it.

Basis: See *Tax basis.*

Beneficiary: A person or organization who inherits property under the terms of a will, trust, or life insurance policy.

Beneficiary deed: See *Transfer-on-death deed.*

Bequeath: A legal term sometimes used in wills that means "leave"—for example, "I bequeath my diamond brooch to my daughter, Elizabeth Jenkins."

Bequest: The legal term for personal property (that's anything but real estate) left in a will.

Bond: A kind of insurance policy for executors, trustees, and guardians, who are in charge of other people's money. If they wrongfully deprive a beneficiary of property, the bonding company will replace it, up to the limits of the bond. These days, most wills state that the executor does not have to post a bond.

Charitable remainder trust: A kind of trust that allows you to make a gift to a charity during your life and get in return both annual income and, after your death, estate tax savings.

Codicil: A supplement or addition to a will. Because a codicil changes a will, it must be signed in front of witnesses, just like a will.

Community property: Ten states (listed in Chapter 6) follow a system of law called community property. In those states, very generally, all property acquired by a couple while married is community property, except for gifts to and inheritances by one spouse only, or unless the spouses have signed an agreement to the contrary. If separate property and community property are mixed together (commingled) in a bank account and expenditures made from the account, the goods purchased are usually treated as community property unless they can be specifically linked to separate property.

Community property with right of survivorship: A special way for married couples to hold title to property, available in some community property states. It allows one spouse's half-interest in community property to pass to the surviving spouse without probate.

Costs of administration: Costs of taking a probate proceeding through court, including such expenses as probate court filing fees, attorneys' fees, accountant fees, appraisers' fees, bond premiums, and fees for public notices.

Creditor: For probate purposes, a creditor is any person or entity to whom a deceased person was liable for money at the time of death.

Custodian: Someone authorized to manage property given to or inherited by a child, under laws called the Uniform Transfers to Minors Act or the Uniform Gifts to Minors Act.

Decedent: Someone who has died.

Decree: A court order.

Deed: A document that transfers ownership of a piece of real estate. There are many types of deeds that may be used for different kinds of transfers.

Deed of trust: A special type of deed similar to a mortgage.

Devise: An old legal term that is generally used to refer to real estate left under a will. In some states, the term now applies to any kind of property left by will.

Devisee: A person or entity who inherits real estate under the terms of a will.

Distributees: Another term for heirs and beneficiaries, or the people who inherit a deceased person's assets.

Donee: Someone who receives a gift.

Donor: Someone who gives a gift.

Encumbrances: Debts (for example, mortgages, property taxes, mechanic's liens, judgment liens, deeds of trust, security interests) tied to specific property as collateral.

Equity: The difference between the fair market value of your real estate and personal property and the amount you still owe on it, if any.

Escheat: The legal doctrine under which property belonging to a deceased person with no heirs passes to the state.

Estate: Generally, the property you own when you die. There are different kinds of estates, including your taxable estate (what is subject to tax), your probate estate (what must go through probate), and your net estate (your net worth).

Estate planning: Taking steps, while you're alive, to leave your property to your loved ones with a minimum of fuss, expense, and taxes.

Estate taxes: See *Federal gift and estate tax.*

Executor: The person specified in a will to manage the estate, deal with the probate court, and collect and distribute assets as the will has specified. If there is no will, or no executor nominated under the will, the probate court will appoint such a person, who is usually called the "administrator" of the estate.

Executrix: A term, now rarely used, for a female executor.

Fair market value: That price for which an item of property would be purchased by a willing buyer and sold by a willing seller. All estates are appraised for their fair market value. The result determines whether they qualify for small estate procedures and whether estate taxes are due.

Family allowance: A certain amount of a deceased person's money to which immediate family members are entitled when probate proceedings are begun. The amount is determined by state law and varies greatly from state to state.

Federal gift and estate tax: A tax imposed by the federal government on people who give away or leave large amounts of property. The estate tax is scheduled to be eliminated entirely by 2010. The gift tax will continue, but with an automatic exemption of $1 million, meaning almost no one will ever have to pay it.

Gift: Property passed to another for nothing in return or for substantially less than its actual market value. Any gift of more than a certain amount (currently $12,000) per year to an individual requires a gift tax return and may be subject to the federal gift tax.

Grantor: Someone who creates a trust. Also called trustor or settlor.

Gross estate: For federal estate tax filing purposes, the total of all property you own at death, without regard to any debts or liens against the property or the costs of administering the estate. However, taxes are due only on the value of the property the person actually owned. In some states, the gross estate is used when computing attorneys' fees for probating estates; the lawyer gets a percentage of the gross estate.

Heir: Generally, any person who is entitled by law to inherit if an estate is not completely disposed of under a will or other method of leaving property at death.

Holographic will: An unwitnessed will in which the signature and all significant provisions are in the handwriting of the person making it. Holographic wills are valid in about half the states.

Inheritance tax: A tax imposed by some states on property owned by a deceased person.

Intangible personal property: Property that does not have a physical form but is represented by a document. Stock in a corporation, the right to receive a pension, patents, and copyrights are all examples of intangible personal property.

Inter vivos trust: See *Living trust.*

Intestate: Someone who dies without having made a valid will is said to die "intestate." In that event, the estate is distributed according to the laws governing intestate succession.

Intestate succession: The method by which property is distributed when a person fails to leave a valid will. Each state's law provides that the property be distributed to the closest surviving relatives. The intestate succession laws of the various states are similar, but not identical. In most states, the surviving spouse, children, parents, siblings, nieces and nephews, and next of kin, inherit in that order.

Inventory: A complete listing of all property owned by a deceased person at death. It is filed with the probate court if probate proceedings are begun.

Issue: A term generally meaning all your children and their children down through the generations: grandchildren, great-grandchildren, and so on. A term often used in place of issue is "lineal descendants."

Joint tenancy: A way to hold title to jointly owned real estate or other property. When two or more people own property as joint tenants, and one of them dies, the others automatically become owners of the deceased owner's share. Because of this "right of survivorship," a joint tenancy interest in property does not go through probate.

Legacy: An old legal word meaning a transfer of personal property by will. The more common term for this type of transfer is bequest.

Letters of administration: A document issued by the probate court that appoints someone as the administrator of an estate.

Letters testamentary: The document given to an executor by the probate court, authorizing the executor to settle the estate.

Lien: A legal claim against your property.

Lineal descendants: See *Issue.*

Living trust: A probate-avoidance trust you create while you're alive and which remains under your control. At your death, property held in trust passes directly to the trust beneficiaries, free of probate. Also called "inter vivos" (Latin for "among the living") trusts.

Marital exemption: A deduction allowed by the federal estate tax laws for all property passed to a surviving spouse who is a U.S. citizen. This deduction (which really acts like an exemption) allows anyone, even a billionaire, to pass his entire estate to a surviving spouse without any tax at all.

Marital property: A term used in Wisconsin for certain property owned by a married couple; for practical purposes, it is the Wisconsin version of "community property."

Minor: In almost every state, any person younger than 18 years of age.

Net estate: The value of all property owned at death less liabilities.

Next of kin: The closest relatives (as defined by state law) of a deceased person.

Notary public: Someone authorized by state law to witness signatures on legal documents and sign them as evidence of the signature's validity.

Payable-on-death account: A bank account for which you have named a beneficiary (called a P.O.D. payee). The payee has no rights while you are alive but will inherit the funds, without probate, in the account when you die.

Personal property: Any kind of property except real estate.

Personal representative: A generic title applied to an administrator or executor of an estate. Some states use this term instead of executor or administrator.

Petition: Any document filed with a court requesting a court order. In the probate context, the term normally describes the initial document filed with the probate court requesting that the estate be "probated," subsequent requests by the executor for permission to take certain actions, and a final request to discharge the executor or administrator and close the estate.

Pretermitted (omitted) heir: A child or spouse who is not mentioned in a will and who a court believes was accidentally overlooked by the person who made the will—typically, when a child is born or adopted after the will is made. If the court determines that an heir was pretermitted, that heir is entitled to receive the same share of the estate as she would have had the testator died intestate.

Probate: Generally, the process by which: 1) the authenticity of your will, if any, is established, 2) your executor or administrator is appointed, 3) your debts and taxes are paid, 4) your heirs are identified, and 5) property in your probate estate is distributed according to your will or state intestate succession laws.

Probate estate: All the assets owned at death that require some form of court proceeding before title may be transferred to the heirs. Property that passes automatically at death (property in a trust, life insurance proceeds, or property held in joint tenancy, for example) is not part of the probate estate.

Quasi-community property: If a married couple moves to a community property state, certain property they acquired in their previous home may be considered "quasi-community property." The rules vary from state to state. Quasi-community property is treated just like community property.

Real property: Another term for real estate. It includes land, of course, and things attached to the land such as trees and crops, buildings, and stationary mobile homes. Anything that is not real property is termed personal property. See *Personal property.*

Residence: The place a person considers and treats as home. For example, although senators typically spend most of their time in Washington, D.C., they generally consider the states they come from as their legal residences. With rare exceptions, a person may have only one residence. A deceased person's estate, with the exception of certain property located in other states, is subject to the laws of the state where the person resided at the time of death.

Residuary estate: All the property in the probate estate except for property that is specifically and effectively left to designated beneficiaries.

Securities: Stocks and bonds.

Separate property: In community property states, all property owned by a married person that is not community or quasi-community property. Separate property generally includes all property acquired before the marriage or after a legal separation, property acquired by separate gift or inheritance at any time, property acquired from separate property funds, and property that has been designated separate property by agreement of the spouses.

Succession: Inheriting property under your state's intestate succession law instead of a will.

Successor trustee: The person named in a trust document to take over as trustee after the death or incapacity of the original trustee. With a probate-avoidance living trust, the successor trustee's main job is to distribute trust assets after the original trustee's death.

Summary probate: A relatively simple probate proceeding available to "small estates," as that term is defined by state law. (Every state's definition is different.)

Surviving spouse: A widow or widower.

Tangible personal property: Personal property that takes a tangible form, such as automobiles, furniture, and heirlooms. Although such items as stock ownership and copyrights may be represented by paper certificates, the actual property is considered intangible. See *Intangible personal property.*

Tax basis: The figure used to calculate taxable gain or loss when you sell an item of property. Generally, the amount of your basis is what you paid for the item, or if you inherited it, its market value at the time you acquired it. If you have a basis of $100, and sell the item for $300, you have a taxable gain of $200.

Taxable estate: Property subject to the federal gift and estate tax. It's the fair market value of all assets owned at death (gross estate) less certain allowable deductions, such as debts, last illness and funeral expenses, and expenses of administering the estate.

Tenancy by the entirety: A special kind of joint tenancy that's only for married couples and, in Hawaii and Vermont, to unmarried couples who have registered with the state. It is available in about half the states.

Tenancy in common: A way two or more people can own property together. Each can leave his or her interest upon death to beneficiaries of his choosing instead of to the other owners (as is the case with joint tenancy). Also unlike joint tenancy, the ownership shares need not be equal.

Testate: Someone who dies after making a valid will is said to have died "testate."

Testator: A person who makes a will.

Transfer agent: A representative of a corporation who is authorized to transfer ownership of the corporation's stock from one person to another.

Transfer-on-death deed: A deed, allowed in several states, that takes effect only at the property owner's death. It's a way to leave real estate without probate.

Trust: An arrangement under which one person, called the trustee, holds legal title to property on behalf of another, called the beneficiary. See *Living trust.*

Trustee: The person who has legal authority over assets held in trust. With a simple probate-avoidance trust, the person who creates the trust is also the trustee.

Uniform Gifts to Minors Act: A set of statutes adopted by many states that allows you to appoint a custodian to manage certain kinds of property you give to a minor during your life.

Uniform Transfer-on-Death Securities Act: A statute adopted by most states that allows you to name a beneficiary to inherit your stocks or bonds without probate.

Uniform Transfers to Minors Act: A set of statutes, adopted by most states, which provides a way for someone to give or leave property to a minor by appointing a "custodian" to manage the property for the minor.

Will: A document, signed and witnessed as required by law, in which you state whom you want to inherit your property and name a guardian to raise your young children if it's necessary.

■

INDEX

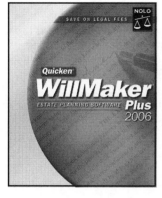

Remember:

Little publishers have big ears.
We really listen to you.

Take 2 Minutes
& Give Us
Your 2 cents

Your comments make a big difference in the development and revision of Nolo books and software. Please take a few minutes and register your Nolo product—and your comments—with us. Not only will your input make a difference, you'll receive special offers available only to registered owners of Nolo products on our newest books and software. Register now by:

PHONE
1-800-728-3555

FAX
1-800-645-0895

EMAIL
cs@nolo.com

or **MAIL** us
this registration card

fold here

Registration Card

NAME _____ DATE _____

ADDRESS _____

_____

CITY _____ STATE _____ ZIP _____

PHONE _____ EMAIL _____

WHERE DID YOU HEAR ABOUT THIS PRODUCT? _____

WHERE DID YOU PURCHASE THIS PRODUCT? _____

DID YOU CONSULT A LAWYER? (PLEASE CIRCLE ONE)   YES   NO   NOT APPLICABLE

DID YOU FIND THIS BOOK HELPFUL?   (VERY)   5   4   3   2   1   (NOT AT ALL)

COMMENTS _____

_____

WAS IT EASY TO USE?   (VERY EASY)   5   4   3   2   1   (VERY DIFFICULT)

We occasionally make our mailing list available to carefully selected companies whose products may be of interest to you.

❑ If you do not wish to receive mailings from these companies, please check this box.

❑ You can quote me in future Nolo promotional materials.
   Daytime phone number _____.

PRAV 6.0